ELEMENTARY DRESSAGE

Other books by Harry Disston:

Equestionnaire
Horse and Rider
Know About Horses
Riding Rhymes
Handbook for the Novice Horseman
Quiz Questions for the U.S. Pony Clubs

ELEMENTARY DRESSAGE

Harry Disston

Illustrations by Sam Savitt

South Brunswick and New York:
A. S. BARNES AND COMPANY
London: THOMAS YOSELOFF LTD

© 1970 by A. S. Barnes and Co., Inc.
Library of Congress Catalogue Card Number: 79-107111

A. S. Barnes and Co., Inc.
Cranbury, New Jersey 08512

Thomas Yoseloff Ltd
108 New Bond Street
London W1Y OQX, England

ISBN 0-498-07591-5
Printed in the United States of America

To my wife,
Katie,
who likes to watch and wants to learn.

Contents

Preface / 9
Acknowledgments / 11
1 What is Dressage? / 15
2 What Does Dressage Accomplish? / 17
3 The Dressage Arena / 19
4 The Basic Requirements / 22
5 Qualities That Apply to All Gaits, Movements, and Figures / 24
6 Details of the Gaits, Movements, and Figures / 27
7 Seat and Hands / 47
8 A Suitable Mount / 52
9 A Plan for Training / 54
10 The Rules of Competition / 71
11 How You Are Scored / 77
12 Preparation for a Competitive Ride / 80
13 Tack / 82
14 Dress / 85
15 A Reader / 87
16 Using the Judge's Scores and Comments to Improve Your Performance / 90

17 Advancing to Higher Levels / 92

18 Summary / 94

Appendixes:

    A. Preliminary, First, and Second Level Tests / 96

    B. Conversion Table: Meters—Yards—Feet—Inches / 115

    C. The Rein Effects / 116

Index / 123

Preface

Dressage is making slow but steady progress in the United States. The progress is due largely to the efforts and encouragement of the United States Equestrian Team, the American Horse Shows Association, the Combined Training Association, and the United States Pony Clubs.

Unhappily, however, there is still much misunderstanding of the term dressage. Those unfamiliar with it think only in terms of haute école as exemplified by Olympic riders and the Spanish Riding School in Vienna. Fox hunters, polo players, and even trail riders tend to keep hands off because they believe that dressage will over-collect their horses; to those interested only in the excitement of equestrian sport, dressage seems dull. On the other hand, you will find prompt and general agreement that basic training is a necessary foundation for all horses, regardless of the use to which they are to be put. The preliminary and first two levels of dressage—although this is not generally recognized and accepted—do, in fact provide the exercises and objectives for precisely the basic and elementary training that all horses should have. Perhaps it would have been wise to refer to the first two or the first three levels of dressage tests in terms more descriptive of what they actually are, such as "training rides," "schooling objectives," "a test of training," or some such instead of "dressage." It was considered.

This book is confined to the preliminary and first two levels of dressage. And these (preliminary and first two levels) are, in turn, arbitrarily defined as "elementary." The coverage is broad and includes a detailed plan for training. The content is not new; the organization and presentation are.

Elementary Dressage contains information, guidance, and suggestions to interest and encourage the uninitiated to enjoy the challenge and satisfaction of producing a basically well-schooled horse, and to assist the more experienced and knowledgeable to progress. It is hoped further that instructors, judges' secretaries, and interested nonriders will find the book helpful.

The inherent shortcomings of the written word are well recognized. There is no effective substitute for personal instruction and practice. A book can be of assistance in seeing a project in perspective, in organization, planning, and study—and for reference. A book can be a good *guide* to accomplishment. I trust that this one is.

Acknowledgments

I wish to express my deep appreciation for their review of the manuscript and for the helpful comments made by: Colonel Charles H. Anderson, Colonel and Mrs. Carl H. Asmis, Mr. Richard D. Collins, Mr. and Mrs. Charles D. Grant, Mr. Victor Hugo-Vidal, Major S. Maxfield Palmer, Mr. Nikolai Pavlenko, Mrs. Howard P. Serrell, Mr. Edgar Staples, Mrs. Richard E. Stokes, Colonel Donald W. Thackeray, and Brigadier General Franklin F. Wing, Jr.

I also wish to thank Encyclopaedia Britannica for permission to reprint material originally prepared by me and appearing ("Horsemanship and Riding") in Volume 11.

ELEMENTARY DRESSAGE

1

What Is Dressage?

Dressage is a method of training horses to meet prescribed standards, emphasizing balance, rhythm, impulsion, calmness with keenness, obedience, collection and extension at certain gaits, performing basic movements and figures—and demonstration of achievement in these areas.

The subject includes: 1) The standards of performance to be achieved; 2) Means of achieving these standards; 3) Tests (prescribed rides) to determine the extent to which the desired standards have been achieved.

From the viewpoint of action, Dressage includes: 1) Gaits, paces, halts, and rein backs; 2) Changes of direction; 3) Figures or patterns; 4) Lateral movement; 5) Transitions; 6) Qualities of the horse (impulsion, balance, obedience, etc.); 7) Position of the rider and control of the horse by the rider.

The standards prescribed vary over a wide range. At the beginning are demonstrations of prompt obedience, a natural balance and cadence both in traveling a straight line and in the precise execution of changes of direction and circles at—in most instances—an "ordinary" and extended walk, trot, and canter. At the top is the graceful, supple, highly coordinated execution of most difficult figures and movements with light, rhythmic gaits, marked collection and extension, and a high degree of balance, and movement on two tracks, found in horses trained for Olympic Grand Prix competition.

In the United States, the accepted progress of dressage standards—from highest to lowest—is defined as:

F.E.I.[1]	Grand Prix
	Intermédiare
	Prix St. Georges
A.H.S.A.[2]	Fourth Level
	Third Level
	Second Level
	First Level
	Preliminary

Tests in the first two levels are used in the dressage phase of preliminary and intermediate competitions sponsored by the U. S. Combined Training Association and in the U. S. Pony Clubs' "B" and "A" rallies.

This book considers dressage only at the preliminary, first, and second levels.

---

[1]. International Equestrian Organization (Fédération Equestre Internationale)
[2]. American Horse Shows Association

2

What Does Dressage Accomplish?

The purpose of elementary dressage is to develop an obedient, calm, reasonably balanced and coordinated and fairly supple horse that moves with some impulsion, cadence, and lightness, accepts the bit, will collect (shorten and raise) and extend its gaits a little at the rider's request. These abilities are demonstrated by the prompt, precise, and smooth execution of certain prescribed gaits, some simple movements, and some simple figures.

The development of the horse's ability through elementary dressage is pursued both as an end in itself and to provide a sound basis for further training in whatever specialized use the horse will be put to—such as hunting, polo, show jumping, trail and pleasure riding, or cutting and reining.

Figure 1. "Calm—Free—Obedient—On the Bit"

3

The Dressage Arena

The arena in which preliminary, first, and second level tests are usually performed is a rectangle 66 feet wide and twice (132 feet) as long (20 meters by 40 meters). It is called the *small* arena. Sometimes, however, the large arena (following) is used for these tests.

Third and fourth level tests and international competition are performed within a longer rectangle, 66 feet wide by 198 feet long (20 meters by 60 meters). It is called the *large* arena.

We shall discuss only the small arena.

The arena is enclosed by a low fence, approximately 16 inches high. This fence is usually constructed in eleven-foot sections of light wood slats. Cinder blocks with poles inserted are effective, inexpensive, and easily moved and stored. A four-foot-wide removable piece is placed at the center of the 66-foot end where the horses will enter. (This is designated "A.")

Alphabetical markers—in accordance with a prescribed pattern—are placed at strategic points along each side of the arena and at each end to indicate where a gait, movement, or figure begins or ends.

The following diagram shows the location of the markers and the distance between them.

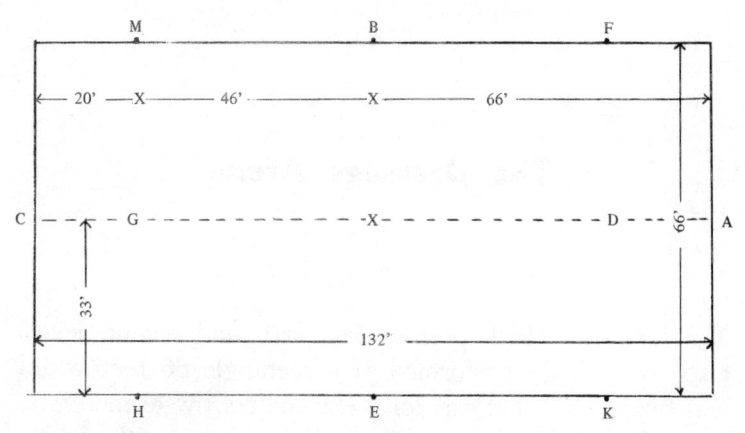

Figure 2. The Dressage Arena—Small

There is no order in the prescribed placement of the letters; the arrangement is arbitrary. It is well at the start to work out some system of association to remember where the letters are in relation to each other. For what it is worth, here is mine. From the judge's position, "C" (the judges *see*), on my left is *M*eadow, *B*rook, *F*oxhounds; on my right H E (C) K! "A" is easy—it's where things start. "X" is in the middle; "D" is closer to "A" than "G" is. After you work in the arena a good deal, the location of the letters will be so well fixed in your mind that a memory prop will no longer be needed.

The three markers on each side and those at each end are usually made of wood or light metal, triangular or square, with the tops about 2½ feet from the ground and the side surfaces ten or twelve inches wide. They rest on the ground or are attached to stakes or poles. The letters, on each side, are painted large enough to be seen from anywhere inside the arena and by the judges.

The judges and secretaries sit on a slightly elevated platform behind "C"; competitors enter at "A."

The center line from "A" to "C" is closely mowed. Sometimes it is marked with lime, but this is not recommended, because of the variation with use. The center point, "X," is clearly marked, and it is well, but not necessary, also to mark "D" and "G." ("D" is on a line with "F" and "K"; "G" is on a line with "M" and "H.")

The arena should, of course, be level and be located, so far as practicable, away from distractions. The long axis should run north and south—if this is at all practicable—with "C," the judges' location, at the south end to avoid the sun in their eyes. Both turf and sand provide good footing.

4

The Basic Requirements

While it must be kept in mind that requirements change from year to year, first level dressage at present requires ability to perform the following:

Halt (stand) immobile five seconds
Ordinary walk
Free walk
Working trot (rising and sitting)
Extended trot (rising and sitting)
Ordinary canter (left and right lead)
Change lead (by moving through the trot)
Move straight down the center line
Turn corners—left and right
Half circle, 33 feet, and return to the track
Circle 26 feet—left and right
Circle 33 feet (half width of the arena)—left and right
Circle 66 feet (width of the arena)—left and right
Change rein (change direction by moving diagonally across the arena)

Second level requires, in addition, these abilities:

Rein back approximately a horse's length
Extended walk
Shoulder-in and straighten
Half turn on the haunches—left and right
Serpentine of 4 loops, width of the arena

Preliminary level tests, added in 1970, include some of the movements and figures of the first level tests (see Appendix A) and are shorter. These two tests are designed to encourage and interest beginning riders with horses of minimum training to participate in Dressage Competitions.

5

Qualities That Apply to All Gaits, Movements, and Figures

To name the gaits, movements, and figures is only a beginning. The important thing is *how* each is to be performed. And this we shall describe. Before proceeding, however, it may be well first to fix in mind the characteristics that apply to all of the gaits, movements, and figures. They are these:

PROMPT   Each movement and figure must begin and end at the designated marker—when the rider's shoulder is at or opposite that point.

PRECISE   The movement or figures must be performed *exactly* as described; a circle is a circle, not an oval; half the width of the arena means just that, half, not a little more or less; an extended trot should be easily distinguished from a working trot; *at* "B" means the change is made neither before nor after "B."

QUALITIES THAT APPLY

STRAIGHT
: When moving on a straight line, the horse's body and movement must be straight; weaving and drifting, and the horse's head carried to the side (when he is traveling a straight line), are faults. At the halt the horse must stand straight on all four legs.

SMOOTH
: This applies primarily to transition from one gait or figure to another and to changes of direction. Too often transitions are abrupt, rough, awkward, and hurried, instead of smooth.

REGULAR
: This applies especially to the gaits. The movement should be in regular beat and time—distinct, cadenced, rhythmic, and steady.

IMPULSION
: There should be evident power in the hind quarters, driving forward with noticeable hock action.

CALM
: The horse must go about his work calmly and relaxed, be on the bit and obedient, while at the same time he is keen and alert. A switching tail, nervously moving ears, and an open mouth indicate resistance and a lack of calmness on the bit.

ON THE BIT
: This means that the horse willingly accepts the bit and is immediately responsive to it. The condition is achieved when the bit is firmly in contact with the bars of the horse's mouth at the end of a taut rein—supple, soft, elastic, and following—giving a good feel of the horse's mouth to the rider's hands. The horse should

neither lean hard against the bit (pull, "bore," "lug") nor attempt to evade it by opening its mouth or placing its head (face) behind the vertical so as to lose contact with it and thus get "behind the bit."

6

Details of the Gaits, Movements, and Figures

Each of the gaits, movements, and figures will now be described in some detail, grouped in four classifications: 1) The Halt, 2) The Gaits, 3) The Movements, 4) The Figures.

THE HALT

At the halt the horse should stand with the weight evenly distributed over its four legs, and be straight, motionless, and alert. The neck is raised, the poll high, the head a little in front of the vertical, the mouth light. The horse may be quietly champing (or mouthing) its bit.

Transition from any gait to the halt is made progressively in a smooth and precise movement. The halt is obtained by displacement of the weight on the quarters by the action of the seat and legs meeting resistance by the hand and bit. In short, the horse is pushed into a restraining bit—not pulled back by the bit.

Usual faults: Not straight, moving, weight uneven, not square, not alert, head too low, resisting, behind the bit.

THE GAITS

Gait and Pace

The two terms are often used interchangeably. This is incorrect. In this book they will be used as follows:
Gait—Basically the gaits are the walk, trot, canter, and gallop. So also are the ordinary walk, trot, and canter; the extended walk, trot, and canter; the collected walk, trot, and canter; and the free walk.
Pace—With one exception (later), pace refers to the speed, regularity, and evenness of a gait (any gait).
Exception—The pace or *a* pace also refers to a two-beat lateral gait characteristic of the Standardbred Horse. It is not so used in this book.

The speed (pace) at which horses travel at the several gaits varies considerably. In general and on the average, however, the pace of the normal or "ordinary" gaits used in dressage are:

GAIT	MILES PER HOUR	1 MILE	1 MINUTE
Walk	4	15 Minutes	117 Yards
Trot	8	7½ Minutes	235 Yards
Canter	12	5 Minutes	352 Yards

The Walk

The walk is a relatively slow (but active) gait of four

beats in which the legs follow one another in four time, well maintained, well marked, even and regular.

It is at the walk that the imperfections in Dressage are most marked. The gait will suffer if the degree of collection is not in accordance with the stage of schooling of the horse.

Ordinary Walk. A regular and unconstrained walk of moderate extension. The horse should walk energetically but calmly, with even and determined steps, distinctly marking four equally spaced beats. The hind feet should follow closely the tracks of the fore feet. The rider should keep a light and steady contact with the mouth.

Common Faults: Failure to maintain a distinct four-beat cadence, variable pace, not straight.

Extended Walk. The horse should cover more ground than at the ordinary walk, without haste and without losing the regularity of its steps. The hind feet touch the ground over or a little beyond the footprints of the fore feet. The rider lets the horse stretch out its head and neck without, however, losing contact; the horse's head is carried in front of the vertical and the rider's hands follow the natural oscillation of the horse's head and neck.

Common Faults: Same as those noted under "ordinary walk," and, in addition, no or very little extension, little difference from ordinary walk, faster rather than extended.

Free Walk. The free walk is a gait of relaxation, where the horse is encouraged to lengthen his stride and achieve complete freedom of the head and neck as the rider maintains only minimum contact.

Common Faults: Same as those noted under "ordinary walk," and, in addition, jigging, variable pace, not relaxed, head and neck not stretched, stride not lengthened, contact too strong, reins too loose, loss of impulsion.

Figure 3. **The Free Walk**

The Trot

The trot is a gait of two beats on alternate diagonals (near fore and off hind and vice-versa), separated by a moment of suspension.

The trot, always with free, active, and regular steps, should be assumed without hesitation.

The quality of the trot is judged by the elasticity and

regularity of the steps and the impulsion, while maintaining a regular cadence.

Ordinary Trot. The Ordinary Trot is no longer called for in the first two levels of dressage. It is included in the third and fourth levels. Until 1970, however, the Ordinary Trot was included in the first two levels. In 1970 the "Working Trot" was substituted for the Ordinary Trot in order to permit progression to that more demanding gait. The Working Trot here follows the Ordinary Trot, which is also included for reference.

This is at a pace between the extended and the collected trot. The horse goes forward freely and straight, engaging his hind legs with good hock action, on a taut but light rein, his position balanced and unconstrained. The steps should be as even as possible. The hind feet touch the ground in the footprints of the fore feet.

The degree of energy and impulsion displayed at the ordinary trot denotes clearly the degree of suppleness and balance of the horse.

Common Faults: Not straight, hind legs inactive or drag, unbalanced, irregular cadence (rhythm).

Working Trot. This pace at the trot is that at which a horse with little training can best carry its rider and itself without special strain (naturally) and is responsive to the rider's aids. It is a little slower and less extended than the Ordinary Trot (described above) but faster and covers more ground than a collected trot. The horse moves at a natural pace in good balance.

The Working Trot provides the foundation for training leading to correct performance of the Ordinary Trot.

Extended Trot. At this pace the stride is lengthened without loss of rhythm or balance. This is preliminary to the horse's being sufficiently trained to be asked to per-

Figure 4a. **The Working Trot**

form a correct extended trot, i.e., before the training has reached a sufficiently advanced stage to produce the impulsion of the hind legs necessary for the extended trot. The stride is lengthened without loss of rhythm.

Common faults: Same as those noted under Working Trot, and, in addition, no or very little extension, faster but no extension, lacks impulsion.

In most movements requiring the Working Trot, the rider sits; where an Extended Trot is called for, the rider is usually required to rise to the trot; but keep in mind that there are exceptions. In some tests, a movement may call for rising at the Working Trot and sitting at the Extended Trot.

Figure 4b. The Extended Trot

The Canter

The canter is a gait of three beats. On the right lead at the canter for instance, the sequence is as follows: left hindleg, left diagonal (right hind and left foreleg), right foreleg followed by a period of suspension with all four legs in the air before taking the next stride.

Ordinary Canter. This is at a pace between the extended canter and the collected canter. The horse, perfectly straight from head to tail, moves freely with a natural balance. The strides are long and even, and the pace well cadenced. The quarters develop an increasing impulsion.

Common Faults: Not straight, unbalanced, disunited (hind out of phase with fore), uneven stride, irregular pace, "four-beat canter" (no distinct period of suspension).

The collected and extended canter are not called for in the first two levels.

Change of Lead or Leg at the Canter

This is a change whereby the horse is brought down to a trot and, after several strides at the trot, is restarted into a canter with the other leg leading.

Common Faults: Failure to change through the trot, change abrupt or rough, not straight, horse resisting or excited.

THE MOVEMENTS

The Rein Back

The rein back is a backward movement, the legs being raised and set down simultaneously by diagonal pairs. The horse should move regularly in two time, the hind legs remaining well in line and the legs being well raised. The horse must be ready to halt or move forward without pausing at the demand of his rider, remaining at all times lightly on the bit and well balanced.

Hurrying, evasion of the hand, deviation of the quarters

from the straight line, or spreading and inactivity of the haunches are serious faults. Violent influence on the part of the rider may be detrimental to the joints of the hind quarters. A horse that is not obedient to the aids of the rider in the rein back is insufficiently suppled, badly schooled, or badly ridden.

If, in a Dressage test, a trot or a canter is required after

Figure 5. **The Rein Back**

a halt or a rein back, the horse must strike off immediately into this pace without an intermediate step.

Common Faults: Resisting, dragging (instead of stepping) back, uneven and uncadenced steps, not straight, too few and too many steps, hurrying, not moving off immediately to the next required gait.

Turn on the Haunches

This is schooling exercise executed from the halt or walk. Initially the hind legs are allowed to describe a small circle (half circle) in conjunction with ranging of the forehand. As training progresses the small circle is reduced in diameter until the horse's forehand moves in even, quiet, and regular steps around the horse's active inner hind leg. This movement may be executed through 90°, 180°, or 360°. When done from the walk, the movement is executed in the same manner as above, but without the definite halt; the horse is taken fluently from the walk into the turn on the haunches. The half turn is 180°.

Common Faults: Stepping backward, circle or half circle described by the hind legs two wide or too large, turn partially on the forehand; when executed from a walk, a change or hesitation in the gait before making the turn, fixed hind leg.

Shoulder-In

Shoulder-In is the foundation of other lateral movements. The horse is bent around the inside leg of the rider (toward the center of the arena) and moves nearly —but not actually—on two tracks. The outside shoulder is placed in front of the inside hind quarter. The inside legs

DETAILS 37

Figure 6. Turn on the Haunches—Pattern of Hind Feet

pass and cross in front of the outside legs. The horse's body is bent away from the direction to which he is moving, but *not more than 45°*.

The bend of the horse is more or less accentuated according to the degree of lateral suppleness the rider seeks to attain. Above all, impulsion must be maintained.

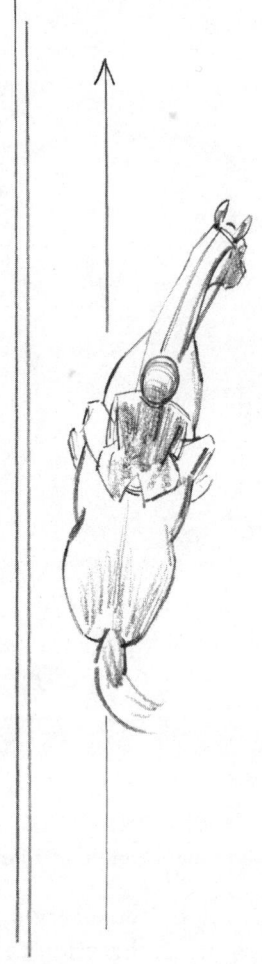

Figure 7. Shoulder-In, Right

Common Faults: Only the neck and head are bent, not the body; the horse's body bent substantially less or more than 45°, loss of impulsion, loss of gait, variable pace, inside leg does not cross in front of outside leg.

Transitions—Change of Gait and Pace (Speed)

Such changes should be made promptly and yet be smooth and not abrupt. The cadence of a gait should be maintained up to the moment when the gait is changed or the horse halts. The horse remains light in hand and calm and maintains a correct position.

THE FIGURES

Down Center Line

In moving down the center line—always at the beginning and end of a test ride—it is necessary, first, to move *straight*. A common fault is to "weave." The regularity, freedom, and impulsion of the gait must be maintained.

Corners

Ride straight to the corner on the track, make a smooth turn without hesitation and without change of pace or cadence and continue on the track at a right angle to the track you left. The horse must be flexible, the spine and neck bent in the direction of the turn. The hind legs follow the track of the fore legs. At "ordinary" gaits, the diameter of the half circle would be 18 to 20 feet. The rider's shoulders are parallel to the horse's shoulders.

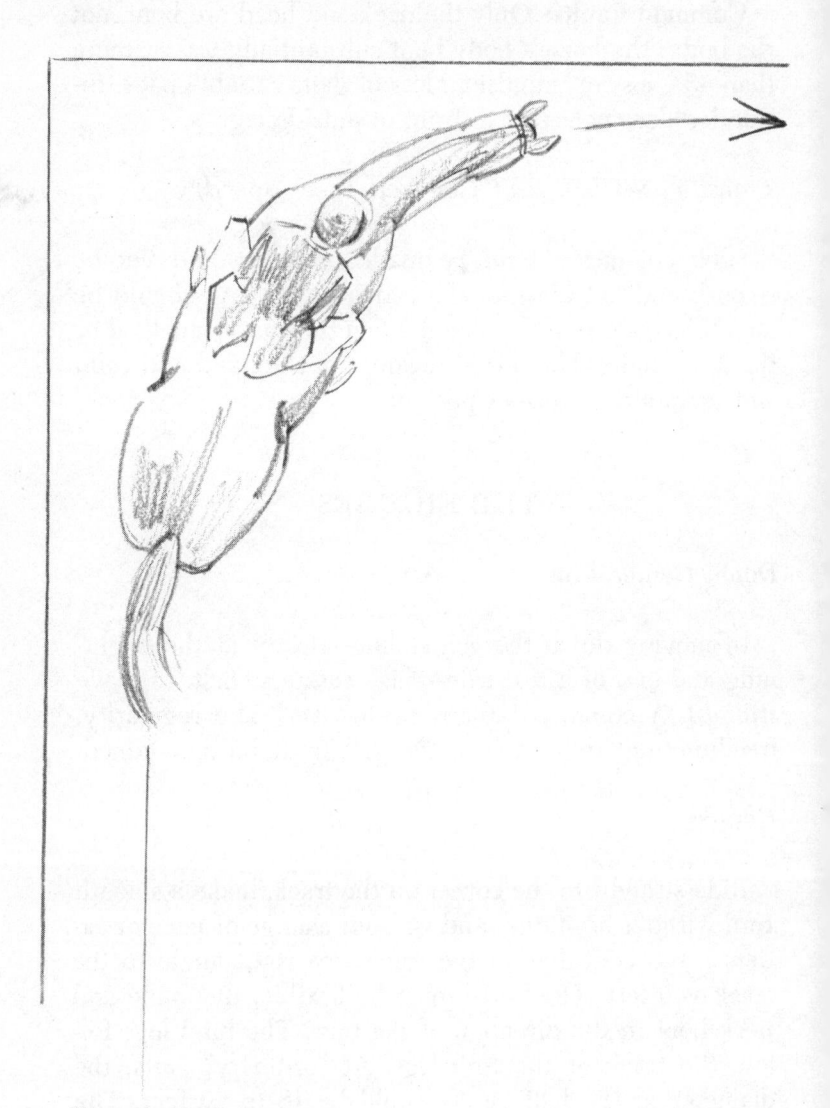

Figure 8. Turning a Corner

Common faults are "cutting" the corners, square corners, hesitating and losing impulsion and pace, no bend.

Circles

The circles required in first and second level dressage are: 26 feet in diameter, 33 feet (half the width of the arena), and 66 feet (the width of the arena).

Circles require attention in three areas—riding precisely the trace of the circle required, transition to the circle at the letter designated, maintenance of the gait and pace called for and impulsion. Learning to ride precisely the trace of the true circle requires training aids and much practice. You need to concentrate both on a precise circle and maintenance of pace and impulsion.

Faults in performance of circles are found in all three of the areas mentioned above, but most, perhaps, in an irregular trace or a circle too small or too large, and in loss of impulsion. A serious fault is the horse's carrying its head to the outside of the circle with its body not properly bent to the inside.

Half Circle and Return to the Track

The half circle—started at one of the four letters near the end or short side—and return to the track at a designated letter—normally the one midway on the long side where the half circle is made (E or B) requires the same attention as the circle itself—precision, proper transition, and maintenance of pace, cadence, and impulsion.

As a rule, in the half circles and return to the track in first and second level tests, the half circles are 33 feet in diameter.

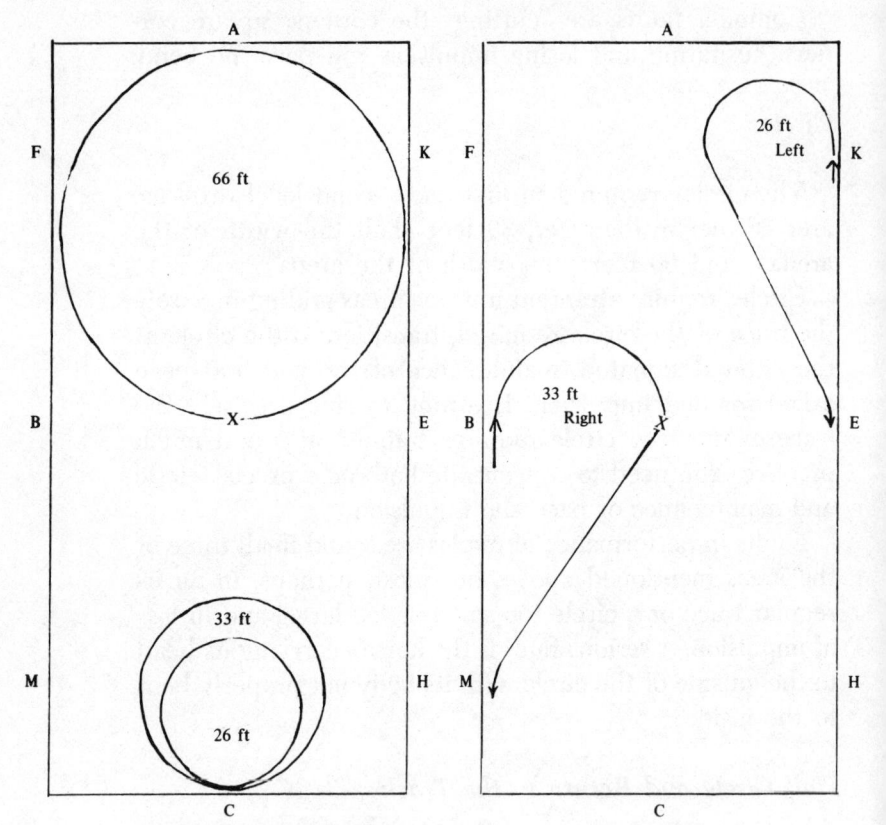

Figure 9. Circles and Half Circles Returning to the Track

The most common faults are, understandably, poor execution of the half circle, insufficient bend, loss of cadence, lack of precision.

Serpentines

These are a series of equal curves from one side of the center line to the other, designed to demonstrate supple-

DETAILS 43

ness in bending and straightening. The number of curves, as well as their size, is prescribed in tests. The first loop is commenced at the center of one of the ends (A or C);

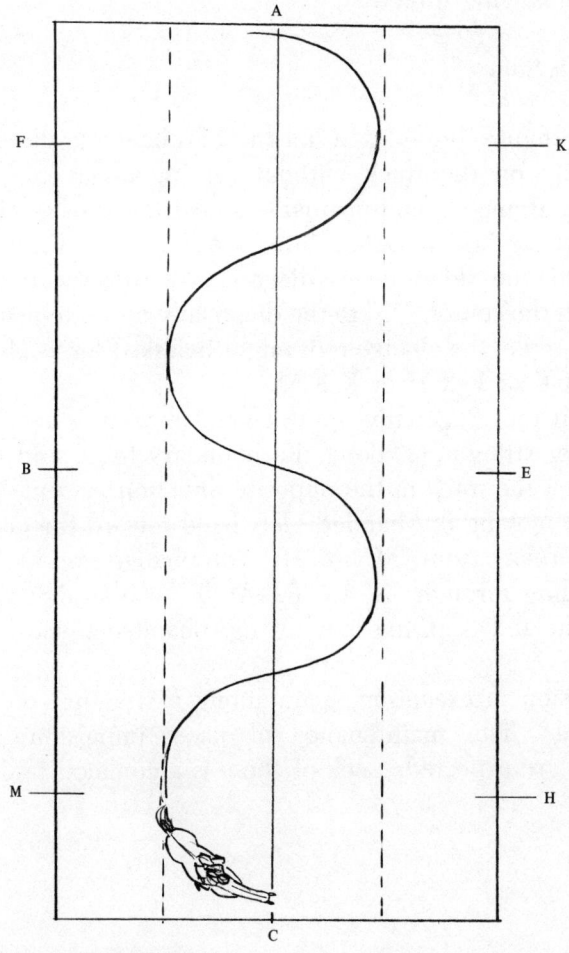

Figure 10. **Serpentine**

the horse then continues through the number loops to the opposite end (C or A) and finishes facing in the direction of the next movement.

Common Faults: Curves too large, too small, too many, too few; irregular curves, variable pace, loss of impulsion when changing direction.

Change Rein

This figure provides a means of changing direction smoothly on the track without turning about. It commences at one of the four markers near the ends of either side, "H" or "M" or "K" or "F." (See Figure 2.) From one of these, the rider moves diagonally across the arena—through the center, "X," to the diagonally opposite marker. For example, the change rein might be asked for as H-X-F or M-X-K or F-X-H or K-X-M.

When the diagonally opposite end marker is reached, the rider straightens along the boundary fence and continues on the track in the opposite direction. Assume that you are moving *left*-handed (left hand toward the center of the arena) from "M" to "H." You change rein at "H," proceeding through "X" to "F." At "F" you straighten to the right and continue moving *right*-handed toward "A" and "K."

Precision in execution, maintaining a straight (on the diagonal) line, maintenance of pace, impulsion, and rhythm are expected. Lack of these is a common fault.

DETAILS 45

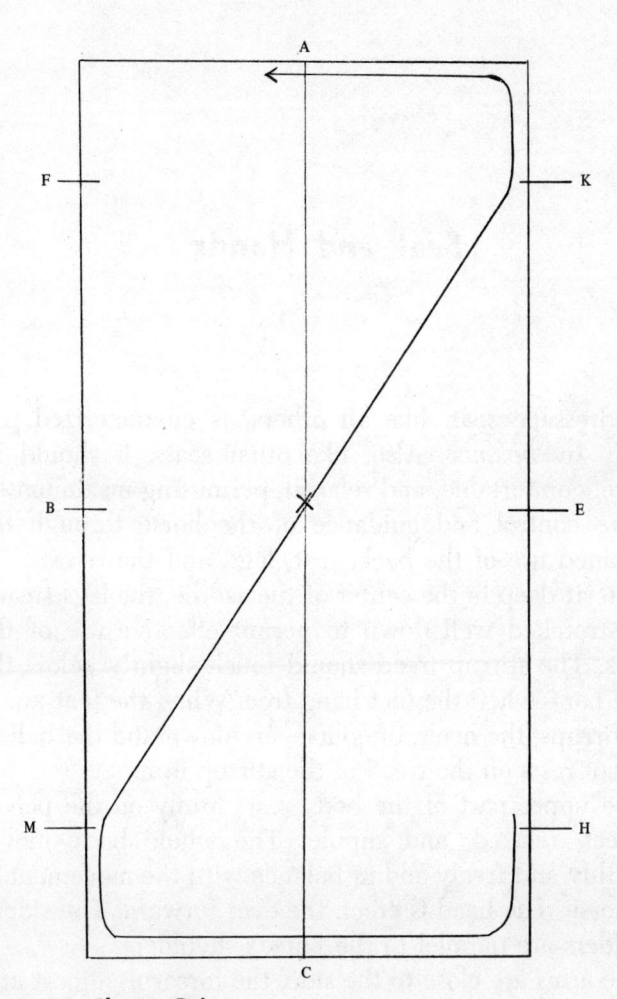

Figure 11. Change Rein

7

Seat and Hands

The dressage seat, like all others, is characterized primarily by *balance*. Also, like other seats, it should be secure, comfortable, and relaxed, permitting maximum effective control and guidance of the horse through the combined use of the back, seat, legs, and the reins.

You sit deep in the center of the saddle, the legs steady and stretched well down to permit effective use of the calves. The stirrup tread should touch slightly below the ankle bone when the feet hang free. When the feet are in the stirrups, the heels, of course, are down and the ball of the foot rests on the tread of the stirrup iron.

The upper part of the body rests firmly on the pelvis, is erect, relaxed, and supple. The whole body moves smoothly and freely and in balance with the movement of the horse. The head is erect, the eyes forward. The rider's shoulders are parallel to the horse's shoulders.

The arms are close to the side, the forearms almost at a right angle with the upper arms. The hands are about a hand's height above the withers and about 6 inches in front of the body so that there is a straight line from the rider's elbows to the rings of the (snaffle) bit. The hands are fairly close together, the thumbs up and pointed toward each other (you must use both hands). The hands are relaxed and active, always in contact through the rein with the horse's mouth.

At the canter, you sit constantly in the saddle, the upper body quiet.

The object of a good dressage seat is to push the horse continuously forward through the influence of the back, seat, and legs with quiet hands and both legs providing steady and steadying contact—and all of this unobtrusively.

Figure 12. The Dressage Seat

SEAT AND HANDS 49

Figure 13a. **Hunter Seat**

Figure 13b. Saddle Seat

SEAT AND HANDS 51

Figure 13c. **Stock Seat**

8

A Suitable Mount

The qualities and characteristics desirable for elementary dressage will be found in many horses and, I dare say, in most. Success depends almost wholly on the intelligence and skill of the trainer and the regularity of the training the horse receives.

You will want a horse that is sound, well coordinated, a free mover, keen and alert, and with a calm temperament. One with these characteristics might seem hard to find, but there are many.

In height and weight, the horse should suit the rider. As a rule, the height should be from 15.0 to 16.1 hands. While, of course, there are exceptions, small horses and ponies tend to have "mincey," shortened gaits and very large horses are apt to be awkward. Similarly, horses with very short and very long backs are apt not to move as well as those with "normal" length backs.

A horse that is too round barreled, wide chested, and "mutton shouldered" is not only apt to be a poor mover, but also causes some difficulty in applying the leg aids. A neck can hardly be too long; one too short and thick is a liability. The main thing is that the horse be in proper proportion to its height.

Any breed will do. Thoroughbreds and Half Thoroughbreds appear to be seen more than other breeds in advanced dressage, but almost every breed *is* represented. In considering a Thoroughbred or an Arabian, give special attention to temperament. Some individuals of these two breeds tend to be a little "hot" or unduly excitable if not in the hands of a skilled and experienced trainer.

A most important consideration in selecting your horse is in what other capacity it will be used. This might well be the deciding factor.

Figure 14. **A Suitable Mount—Side, Front, and Rear Views**

9

A Plan for Training

Your overall plan for training can be simplified and concentrated to advantage by dividing it into four distinct and natural phases:
> The Halt
> The Gaits and Paces
> The Rein Back, the Turn on the Haunches, and Shoulder-In
> The Figures

Start all of your planning and each training session with a review of the objective and the detailed requirements of the gait, pace, movement, or figure with which you are working—and have these clearly in mind throughout.

Spurs provide a desirable and useful reinforcement of the leg aids.

Let us now consider a plan or a routine or a procedure, whichever you wish, for each of the "movements" included in each of the four broad classifications—and some training aids that might prove helpful.

The Halt. In your training area, select a post, stake,

marker, or any other easily identified spot—or better, several of them—at which to practice executing the halt, and vary them so the horse will not anticipate. In addition, if you have nearby bridle trails available, pick out certain definite spots along the trail to practice the halt—but not the *same* ones.

It is important to start your training in dressage with the halt, because it is difficult and, in the normal course of riding, you halt often. Your horse will necessarily develop the habit of a good or a poor halt. Standing straight, immobile, balanced, square, and alert is not easy; to achieve this requires the trainer to be intelligent, knowledgeable, understanding, persistent, and patient.

Remember the basic principle—that the halt is achieved by urging the horse forward with your legs into a resisting or restraining bit—not by pulling the horse back.

Practice the halt at a specified, but varied, point using the legs and hands as described above. When the horse responds by coming to a stop standing straight, reward him by relaxing pressure on the bit. Now count "one thousand one, one thousand two," and so on to "one thousand five." This should consume about 5 seconds—but vary this.

If the horse attempts to move backward, apply the legs and keep a firm hand on the bit. If he is not standing straight or attempts to move to one or the other side, use a strong leg (pressure) on the side to which he slants.

Each time your horse stands still for 5 seconds and straight, reward him with encouraging words and a pat.

Sometimes you will be aware of it, but more often you will need a "ground man," a coach, to tell you if your horse is standing square and balanced—and what to do if he is not.

Last, when your horse has learned well the other requirements, teach him to be and to remain alert and attentive. Constant, even, light contact with your legs and a slight, almost imperceptible play of the bit will accomplish this.

Ordinary Walk. While you are mastering the halt, you may also work on the Ordinary Walk.

The basic and essential effort here is to keep pressing the horse into the bit with your legs. Light contact of a flexible and sensitive hand is needed to maintain an even, regular, cadenced, well-marked four-beat stride of moderate length. And, again, you must use your legs and the reins to keep your horse moving straight. At the Ordinary Walk, the hind feet should be planted about where the fore feet were.

A carefully measured distance along a nearly straight line on reasonably level ground providing good footing is a valuable aid in developing an even, regular, and cadenced (rhythmic) stride.

A free-moving horse, 15 to 16 hands high, is likely to walk naturally—neither collected nor extended—about 4 miles per hour. Some, of course, will walk naturally at a pace of 4½ or 5 miles per hour. Before proceeding with your training at the Ordinary Walk, determine your horse's natural pace—and do not restrict it. If the horse tends to be slow, sluggish, and hesitant, you must teach it to walk freely at least 4 miles per hour. If it is a free mover and has a naturally long stride, train it to maintain this at an even pace.

Let us continue the discussion, however, on the assumption that your horse walks naturally and freely at 4 miles per hour—a mile in 15 minutes. This will facilitate—and is only for the purpose of—illustration.

If you have a suitable trail or path a mile long, that is great. But even so, you will want to mark at least each eighth of a mile (furlong) to check the evenness and regularity of your pace. If, as so often is the case, your training area is restricted, you can lay out a quadrangle 200 yards long and 20 yards wide. Once around this is 440 yards or a quarter of a mile. You will have the additional training value of teaching your horse and yourself *not* to cut corners! If necessary, you can lay out a smaller quadrangle, 100 yards by 10 yards, providing an eighth of a mile (furlong) circuit. If your available area limits you to it, you may design a 110-yard straight path and ride it back and forth.

You can, indeed, time yourself in negotiating the known distances, but this is very distracting. It is best to have a "ground man" time you, preferably with a good stop watch. Assuming a mile in 15 minutes, you should cover an eighth of a mile in 113 (or 112) seconds (1 minute 53 (or 52) seconds), a quarter mile in 225 seconds (3 minutes, 45 seconds). After considerable training over timed known-distance courses, you will become proficient in judging correct pace and sensitive to variations in it.

Extended Walk. When your horse has learned to perform the Ordinary Walk satisfactorily, start to teach him the Extended Walk. The Extended Walk requires a lengthened stride—the hind feet planted slightly ahead of where the front feet were. The pace (speed) rgularity and cadence do not change. The horse simply walks with a longer stride.

The lengthening of the stride is obtained by increased pressure of the legs without relaxing the light and steady contact through the bit.

Since your horse is covering a little more ground with each stride, he will cover a mile in from 1 to 2 minutes less than at the Ordinary Walk (a mile in 13 to 14 minutes).

Free Walk. At the Free Walk, your horse should noticeably lower his head and stretch his neck (while you too let the reins "stretch") while taking up about the same lengthened stride as in the Extended Walk. The horse should be relaxed and calm, but still maintain the evenness, regularity, and cadence of the gait. Contact with the horse's mouth is minimum.

In your schooling sessions, it is well frequently to alternate moving from the Ordinary Walk to the Extended Walk and then to the Free Walk and starting with the Extended Walk to move successively to the Ordinary Walk and then the Free Walk. At all times, pay particular attention that your horse is moving *straight*.

Working Trot. Review and have clearly in mind the requirements of the Working Trot as described in Chapter 6. Proceed in your training in a manner similar to that used for the Ordinary Walk. The challenge is to use your legs, back, seat, and reins to keep your horse straight and to maintain an even, regular, cadenced pace—with some show of impulsion while remaining calm.

Here, again, you will find the known-distance pacing strip or track useful in obtaining and checking the pace of your trot. The speed at the Ordinary Trot of the average horse is about 8 miles per hour (a mile in 7½ minutes). Rarely would it be slower than this, but in a number of instances it might be more—up to 9 miles an hour.

Change frequently from the Working Trot to the Ordinary Walk and vice-versa, emphasizing smooth transition.

Extended Trot. Review and have clearly in mind the requirements of the Extended Trot as described in Chapter 6. Proceed with your training in a manner similar to that used for the Extended Walk. You need especially to remember that the task is to lengthen the stride without increasing the cadence.

Because of the greater amount of ground covered with each stride, the speed of the Extended Trot—for a horse whose Working Trot is 8 miles per hour—would be from 8½ to 9 miles per hour (a mile in 7.1 to 6⅔ minutes). Relative to various speeds at the Working Trot, the Extended Trot might be anywhere from 8½ to perhaps 10 miles per hour.

Change from the Extended Trot to the Working Trot and then to the Ordinary Walk and the reverse, emphasizing smooth transitions.

Ordinary Canter. In addition to the basics of moving straight on one track and maintaining the gait at an even, regular, and cadenced pace, the challenge at the canter is to train your horse to take willingly and promptly the lead you desire.

To make it easy and natural for your horse to take the correct lead promptly and to associate your aids with it, start your training in the canter from the trot on a fairly small circle (26 feet to 33 feet in diameter).

Use the diagonal aids—the rein in indirect opposition in front of the withers on the side he is to lead and a strong outside leg. For example, to canter on the *left* lead from the trot on a circle:

Raise the left hand slightly and carry it to the right across the horse's neck, applying pressure to the right rear (left indirect rein of opposition in front of the withers); the horse's muzzle will be turned slightly to the left. This weights and restrains the right shoulder while freeing the left shoulder and permitting its extension.

With the right hand, apply a slight pressure straight to the rear (direct rein of opposition) to assist the action of the left rein and to steady the horse.

Apply strong pressure with the right leg behind the girth to move the haunches to the left and cause the left lateral to lead the right.

Apply a slight pressure with the left leg at the girth to assist the right leg in producing increased impulsion and to prevent too great a displacement of the haunches to the left.

With both reins restrain slightly the increased impulsion provided by the legs to "lift" the horse's forehand; then, as the left leg extends, yield the hands slightly.

When your horse has learned to canter willingly and promptly on both leads from a trot on a circle, start training him to depart on either lead (willingly and promptly) from a walk and on a straight line.

If your horse resists, hesitates, or departs on an incorrect lead, *immediately* return him to the trot or walk and start over again.

Vary considerably and frequently the place and time you take up the canter and where and when you canter on a desired lead and where and when you change, along with the length of time or distance you maintain the canter. Your horse is apt to think that a specific area, stretch of path, or specific point is the place where he should canter on a specific lead unless you vary these locations.

After you have achieved a willing and prompt depart on either lead from a trot and a walk, concentrate on keeping your horse moving straight at the canter. (There is a tendency in most horses to throw their haunches from side to side and to move on two tracks). Work also on the evenness and regularity of the gait.

The pace, at the Ordinary Canter, for most horses is about 12 miles per hour (a mile in 5 minutes); for some, it might be 12 to 14 miles per hour.

Change of Lead (Leg). This is accomplished first by bringing your horse from the canter back to the trot for a few strides and then applying the aids to lead with the opposite leg.

For example: If your horse is cantering on a *left* lead, bring him to a trot for two or three (not more) strides and then—with a strong left leg and the right rein in indirect opposition in front of the withers and a shift of your weight from left to right—send your horse into a canter on the *right* lead.

Spend some time assuring yourself that your horse changes *behind* as well as in front.

When your horse responds satisfactorily to your request for a change through the trot, proceed similarly to train him to make the change through one or two well-defined steps at the *walk*. (Only the change through the trot is called for in the first two level tests.)

Rein Back—Many horses learn quickly to rein back willingly and properly, others are very slow in learning this exercise; they resist, drag back unbalanced, scurry backward, and move to one side. Persistence will bring them around, and once having learned to perform correctly they will be consistently good.

The horse is taught to rein back by a procedure similar to that used in obtaining the halt. By pressure of the legs, aided by the back and seat, the horse is moved forward into a restraining bit, but in the case of the rein back the pressure on the bit is greater than at the halt—strong enough to cause the horse to step backward.

At first, work on a willing and prompt response to the aids—just teach the horse to move backward. At this stage, too, use the bit to cause your horse to bend at the poll. (Many respond to the aids by stepping backward, but, at the same time, poke their muzzles forward—that is, they bring their heads *up* instead of bending at the poll.)

When you have accomplished a willing and prompt backward movement in response to the aids, begin to teach your horse to move straight back in even, regular, and distinct steps, maintaining balance.

Strong pressure by the leg on the side that is moving away from a straight line is the obvious and eventual remedy. It may be helpful, however, to accustom your horse to the idea from the start by backing him through a narrow chute that will permit little deviation. The chute should be 20 to 24 feet long. An existing fence can be one side. Jump standards, sections of post and rail fence, or easily built board fencing (20 to 24 feet long) may form the other side. The width of the chute would be 3 feet to 3½ feet, depending on the width of the horse. You would back through in one direction, then turn about and back through in the opposite direction.

Even, regular, and defined steps are obtained by: 1) keeping your legs on the horse so that its hocks are under it and, 2) relaxing a little the pressure on the bit after each step and then resuming it for the next step—a take and give at each step. Your horse should bend at the poll, but you need to be careful that it is not *overflexed*—that its face does not come behind the vertical.

After the exercises outlined above have achieved a satisfactory result, practice halting and backing a determined number of steps (4, 5, or 6) at a specific point (a fence post, a tree, an arena marker) as with the plan used to practice the halt. After the determined number of steps has been taken, alternate standing quietly for 3 seconds and then moving off with moving off without hesitation at an Ordinary Walk. When this transition is mastered, move off—following the halt after the rein back—at a Working Trot.

Last, practice smooth transition from the three gaits to the *halt*, then rein back 4 steps, then move off promptly at a walk or a trot.

Half Turn on the Haunches—(A turn about of 180°.) This is a difficult movement; it requires a skilled rider and an obedient and reasonably well-schooled horse. The problem is to keep the horse from moving either forward or backward, and especially to prevent the horse from moving its hind quarters outside away from what should be the pivot—the inside hind foot.

Review and keep the requirements of the movement clearly in mind.

The keys to this movement are: 1) fixing the hindquarters as the pivot (strong pressure from the outside leg), 2) preventing the horse from backing (use of the inside leg if the horse attempts it), and 3) the displacement of the shoulders about the haunches as a pivot (direct and indirect reins of opposition).

It will help in the initial stages of training in this movement to start from alongside a fence or wall—the horse's right side parallel to it when you practice turning left, his left side parallel to it when you practice turning right. Start with a quarter turn.

To turn to the left, with both legs press the horse into the bit and apply only enough pressure on the bit to move the weight to the hindquarters without causing the horse to back and apply the direct rein of opposition on the left, the indirect rein of opposition in front of the withers on the right. Apply a strong right leg to prevent the haunches from displacing to the right and apply the inside leg, the left, at the girth, to keep the horse pressed into the bit and to keep the hindquarters active.

Shoulder-In. This suppling movement is performed at a walk and at a trot.

The important thing is that the horse's entire body be bent in the direction desired (right or left) at an angle of about 45° (and in no case less than 30°), while at the same time he moves freely and evenly forward with impulsion. The most pronounced bend is at the poll and just in rear of the withers.

If the Shoulder-In is performed to the right, the right hind foot follows in the track of the left fore, and the right feet cross in front of the left. The rider should see the full bulge of the horse's right eye.

To obtain a Shoulder-In to the right, the aids are used as follows:

Shorten the right rein and with the right leading rein *start* your horse on a right turn, moving the horse's shoulders off a straight line. While pressure from both legs is required to preserve forward motion, increased pressure of the right leg behind the girth will assist the turning action of the right rein. (The left leg may have to be used behind the girth to keep the haunches from swinging to the left.)

As soon as your horse is bent to the right and in an oblique position to the straight line you had been traveling, maintain this position as you continue to move forward in the original direction. See Figure 7.

Incline your weight slightly to the left and a little forward (in the direction of movement).

It is well to start training for this movement on a 33-foot circle at a walk, performing the Shoulder-In to the inside. Then progress to practicing the movement along a fence line (the Shoulder-In of course, away from it).

After your horse performs satisfactorily at the walk, move into the trot, first sitting, then posting. In some cases, however, where the horse is slow in responding, it may prove effective to *start* the training in Shoulder-In at the *trot*. This assures maintaining impulsion—difficult to accomplish in a young or green horse.

As your horse improves, work on maintaining impulsion and pace with a pronounced bend.

You accomplish this by applying the right indirect rein

of opposition in front of the withers and a strong right leg. Use the left rein to control and limit the bend of the neck; use the left leg to maintain impulsion and forward movement, and, if necessary, to prevent the haunches from swinging to the left.

In scheduling your training, it might be well to place practice of the Shoulder-In after work on the Circles, Half Circles, and the Serpentine.

Circles. Circles, in first and second level tests, are required with diameters of 26, 33 and 66 feet. Thirty-three feet is half the width of the arena, 66 feet the width of the arena.

Circles need to be ridden with an even and regular pace at the gait required—and, in addition, with precision. This means that the circle is expected to be a *circle*. Too often it is egg shaped, flat, almost square—anything but a circle.

In order to ride a precise circle, you must have in your mind's eye the center of the circle and the four points of a simple +, establishing four points in its circumference. With these four points imagined on the ground, you need only ride a *curved* course between them.

Through other exercises, you have probably trained your horse to a regular, even, and cadenced pace at each gait. In order to achieve a precise circle, you may find it helpful to lay out a "cross" for each of the three sizes of circles—26 feet, 33 feet, and 66 feet—on your training area. This would mean four stakes on the circumference, two at right angles to the other two and one in the center. For example, a 33-foot circle training aid would look like this:

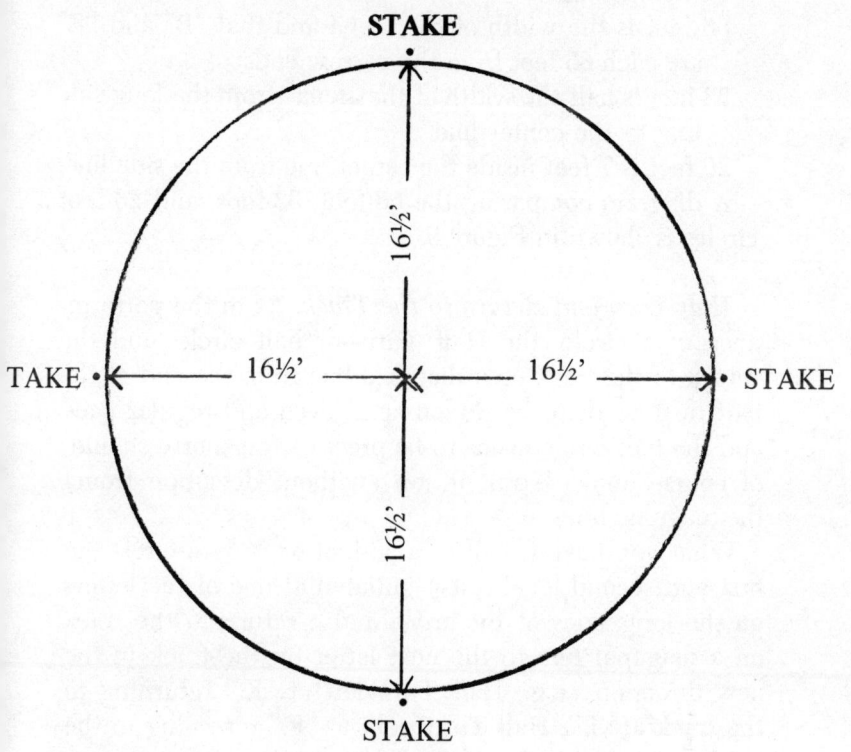

Figure 15. A 33-foot Circle Training Aid

Ride the staked circle frequently in both directions and fix the trace and the five critical points in your mind.

Finally stake the circles in the arena to associate reference points on the center line and the letters along the side.

Measure 16½ feet on either side of "B" and "E" to provide reference points for a 33-foot circle in that area.

Remember that:

66 feet is the width of the arena and that "B" and "E" are each 66 feet from the narrow ends.

33 feet is half the width of the arena—from the long side line to the center line.

26 feet is 7 feet inside the center line from the side line.

A diagram comparing the 66-foot, 33-foot, and 26-foot circles is shown in Figure 9.

Half Turn and Return to the Track. As in the performance of a circle, the Half Turn—or half circle—and the return to the track on a diagonal line from the end of the half turn needs to be ridden at an even and regular pace and the half circle needs to be precise. Your horse should, of course, move "straight" on (without deviation from) the diagonal line.

What you have is half of a 33-foot or 26-foot circle (in first and second level tests) initiated at one of the letters on the long sides of the arena and a return to the track on a diagonal line to the next letter on the track in the new direction (e.g., Half Turn left at "K," returning to the track at "E"; Half Turn right at "F," returning to the track at "B"). See Figure 9.

Before practicing the Half Turn and return to the track, you should be proficient in performing a 26-foot and a 33-foot circle with precision and regularity. Thus, riding half of either of these circles should cause little difficulty. You should also, by this time, be proficient in riding a straight line. Only a little practice then should result in proficient execution of the Half Turn and the return to the track.

Serpentine. In first and second level dressage tests, the

Serpentine usually requires 4 loops the width of the arena or 16 feet 6 inches on each side of the center line. The movement thus takes up the entire width of the arena or half the width of the arena (2 x 16'6" = 33 feet), with the center line running through the middle of the figure. The Serpentine is, in effect, a series of *half* circles in opposing directions. See Figure 10.

The Serpentine is usually performed at a Working Trot. A change of diagonals (by the rider) is made as you cross the center line.

To attain precision in this figure (in addition to regularity and evenness of pace) requires fixing in your mind:
1. The points at which you will cross the center line.
2. The limit of the half circles on either side of the center line.

The Serpentine will start at "A" or "C" and finish at the opposite end of the arena. Therefore, you will *cross* the center line *three* times between "A" and "C." Assume you start at "A," your three crossing points are:
1. Halfway between "A" and "X"
2. "X"
3. Halfway between "X" and "C"

(You will finish at "C"—facing in the direction of the next movement.)

Placing stakes at these critical points will fix them in your mind.

You have, of course, already mastered the Half Circle (or Half Turn).

Change Rein. Correct performance of this figure rests on a prompt, precise, and smooth change of direction at each end of the diagonal ("M" and "K" or "H" and "F") and on riding straight on the diagonal line through "X" without loss of gait, pace, impulsion, or cadence. These features need to be practiced.

Looking ahead to and keeping your eyes on the marker at the far end of the diagonal will assist you in riding straight on it.

10

The Rules of Competition

PRELIMINARY, FIRST, AND SECOND LEVEL

Horses. Conformation is not considered. Marked lameness (sufficient to impair required performance) incurs disqualification.

Bits. In first and second level tests, a *plain snaffle* is required. This may be straight or it may have one or two joints. Types of snaffle bits are pictured in Figure 16.

Noseband may or may not be dropped. (Figure 17 illustrates a dropped noseband.)

Martingales and bearing, side, and running reins are prohibited.

Bandages, boots, and blinkers are prohibited.

Whips are prohibited (except for ladies riding side saddle—rare).

Dress. There is no requirement for the preliminary and first two levels except that it be "proper." It is usual and considered correct, however, to wear: a black (or other dark plain color) coat; a hunting stock and plain pin;

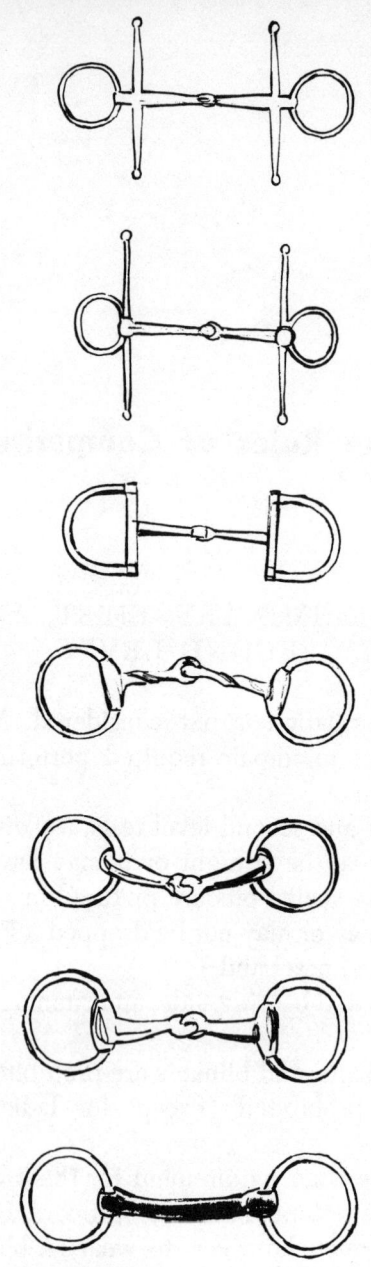

Figure 16. Types of Snaffle Bits

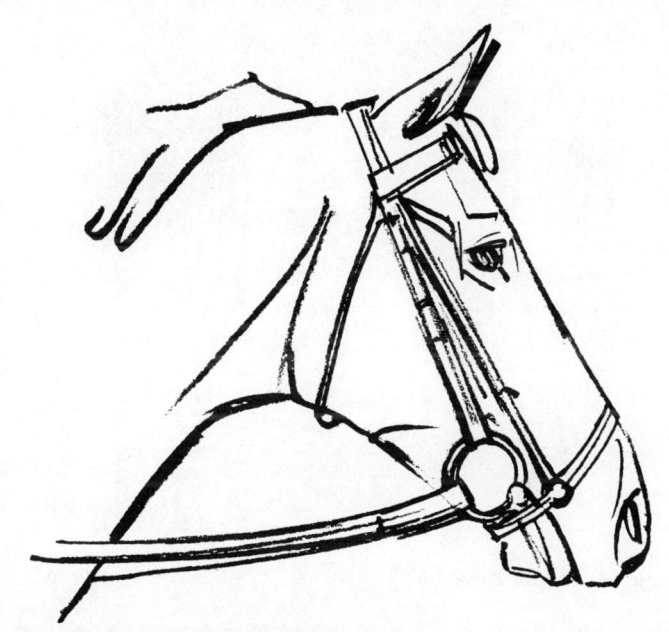

Figure 17. **A Dropped Noseband**

white or canary, buff, light tan, or grey breeches; plain black boots and short shanked spurs; a black or dark blue hunting cap, derby, or, with a "shadbelly" or "pink" coat, a top hat.

Voice. Use of the voice and "clucking" are prohibited. Either is penalized *two points* in each movement where it occurs.

Reading (or announcing). Preliminary, first, and second level rides may be read without penalty—except at final events (where the test must be ridden from memory).

Fall of horse or rider is scored 0 for the movement in which the fall occurs, but the contestant is not eliminated.

Figure 18. **Proper Dress**

If the rider or horse falls outside the arena (during the ride), the fall is penalized by elimination.

Leaving the arena causes elimination. If the horse places *all four* feet outside the fence enclosing the arena he has "left the arena."

Errors in the execution of gaits, paces, movements, and figures are penalized as follows:

> First error, 2 points
> Second error, 5 points
> Third error, elimination

Time. One point is deducted from the score for each *commenced* 5 seconds of time over the time allowed for the ride.

While they will, of course, vary with the content of the

tests, first level tests are usually allowed 6 minutes (in the small arena) and second level tests are usually allowed 7 minutes (in the small arena).

There is no time penalty in the preliminary tests—that is, no prescribed time within which the test must be completed.

Tied Score. In the event of a tied score (where a "ride-off" is not required), the contestant with the higher score under "General Impressions" is declared the winner.

Classification

Preliminary competition is limited to horses that have not twice received a score of 60 percent or more.

First level competition is limited to horses that have not obtained 60 percent or more of the possible score in a first level or higher test prior to January 1 of the current year.

Second level competition is likewise limited to horses that have not obtained 60 percent or more of the possible score in a second level or higher test prior to January 1 of the current year.

These are, however, subject to change from time to time.

Horses may not be entered in classes differing by more than *one* level. For example, a horse may be entered in levels 1 and 2 and 2 and 3, but not 1 and 3.

Summary of Disqualifications:

Marked lameness
Fall *outside* of arena (when performing *in* the arena)
Leaving arena
Three errors

References:

Notes in Dressage and Combined Training—American Horse Shows Association
Rule Book—American Horse Shows Association
Rules for Dressage Competitions of the Fédération Equestre International (F.E.I.)

11

How You Are Scored

In competitive rides, or tests, you are scored by one and sometimes two knowledgeable and experienced judges. The judge will score you 0 to 10 on each of the 12 to 20 movements or phases of the test and on each of four aspects of "General Impressions": 1) Paces—regularity and freedom; 2) Impulsion; 3) Obedience, lightness, and suppleness of the horse; and 4) Position and seat of the rider and correct use of the aids. The total of these individual 16 to 24 scores—less any deductions for errors or for exceeding the time allowed—is your score.

It is helpful in following and appraising your progress to convert the score for each ride into a percentage of "possible" points. For example, if you receive a total score of 108 out of a possible 180, you translate this to 60%; a score of 141 out of a possible 220 becomes 64%.

Here is a description of the points you might receive.

10	Excellent
9	Very good
8	Good

7   Fairly good
6   Satisfactory
5   Sufficient
4   Insufficient
3   Fairly bad
2   Bad
1   Very bad
0   Not performed or fall of horse or rider

Very few judges, it must be observed, score a 10.

Your horse will be judged on the extent to which:

1. He performs the required gaits, movements and figures promptly, precisely, and smoothly.
2. He moves with regularity and freedom and maintains impulsion at all gaits and paces.
3. Transitions from one gait and movement to another are smooth.
4. He stands straight, his weight evenly distributed over the four feet, and immobile at the halt.
5. Moves straight when traveling a straight line.
6. He demonstrates obedience (willing and immediate response to the aids), suppleness, and lightness.
7. Jumps willingly—regardless of style or jumping faults—where jumping an obstacle is required.

You, the rider, are judged on:

1. The correct, smooth, and tactful application of the aids.
2. Unobtrusive application of the aids.
3. Your seat and position.

Remember that:

1. Grinding the teeth (but not champing on the bit), an open mouth, and a swishing tail are considered

evidence of resistance. The tongue over the bit is penalized.

2. A movement is considered correctly commenced at a designated letter if it occurs when the rider's *shoulders* are at that point.
3. The rider is required to use *both* hands (except when rendering the salute to the judge).

Typical comments by judges are:

Not straight	Resisted
Weaved (on center line)	Head behind vertical
Moved (at halt)	Behind bit
Abrupt (or rough) halt	Off balance
Rough transition	Hind legs drag
Transition too late (soon)	No change behind
Lost impulsion	Stiff (not free), restricted
Lacks impulsion	Head bent—no shoulder-in
Aids obvious	Heavy
Irregular (uneven) pace	Sluggish
Cut corner	Disunited
Not extended	Inattentive
Circle irregular	Bucked
Circle too large (small)	Out of control
Rein back hesitant	Bored (lugged)
Hurried	Rose to trot E (Error)

If there are two judges, their scores are added to provide a total score. If the score on any movement differs by more than 2 points, one—or both—of the judges usually modifies his score to bring it within the two-point range.

Refer also to *The Rules for Dressage Competitions*, Chapter 10.

12

Preparation for a Competitive Ride

Before you enter your first competitive ride—presumably a preliminary or first level test—you should be prepared in three areas:

1. You should be able to perform each of the gaits, movements, and figures included in the preliminary or first level tests fairly well. In terms of a score, this would mean that if there was no unforeseen occurrence, your performance would be good enough (by your estimate) to earn a 7, or a 6 at least, from most judges.
2. You should have memorized the two preliminary or first level tests included in the latest edition of *Notes on Dressage and Combined Training* published by The American Horse Shows Association, and have practiced them sufficiently to ride them with confidence and without hesitation.
3. You should relish the opportunity to show how well your horse can do, with full confidence in yourself and your horse.

After your first test ride you will, inevitably, learn that you did not execute some movements as well as you thought you had. Work hard on correcting the weak points developed in your first test and enter another competition. Continue this procedure until—as described in Chapter 17, "Advancing to Higher Levels"—you have received a score of 60 percent or better three times and 75 percent twice. Then go on to the second level tests.

The basic and essential ingredients in preparation for a test are concentration on the individual gaits and movements until they have been mastered and a confident attitude based on this assurance. After that it is learning and benefiting from experience.

13

Tack

The Bit

It is my experience and opinion that a severe bit in light hands is the most effective means of training a horse. It produces instant response. A snaffle bit in unskilled, insensitive, and heavy hands causes a horse to resist by "leaning" on the bit and pulling (boring). A well-schooled horse will, of course, respond readily to the snaffle. There is, however, substantial disagreement on this point. Many experienced horsemen claim that a horse should always receive his early training in a snaffle. Since, in any event, few have really light hands, and since in first and second level dressage tests a snaffle bit is required, the use of a snaffle bit throughout is suggested. The objective is to train your horse to instant and willing response to the *snaffle* bit. Many use a dropped noseband with the snaffle bit. (Figure 17.)

Types of snaffle bits are illustrated in Figure 16.

The Saddle

The saddle should be an "English" or "flat" type of good quality (least expensive in the long run). The seat should be deep (a pronounced pommel and cantle) and of a size to fit you. Usually this would be from 17 to 19 inches, measured from the head of the pommel to the cantle. The size of the saddle depends on the height and weight of the rider and the length of the thigh from hip to knee.

The flaps should be relatively straight or cut only moderately forward, and are better without knee rolls. Neither the exaggerated "forward-seat" jumping saddle nor the saddle-horse show saddle is suitable.

Several manufacturers make a "dressage" saddle, and the type described as an "all-purpose" saddle is also suitable. The typical dressage saddle looks like those on the following page.

Other Items

Bridle and saddle are the only equipment required.

Martingales, side, bearing, and running reins are prohibited in competition. It would be well, therefore, not to use them at any time.

A breastplate would not seem necessary if the horse is normally conformed and if the saddle fits the horse.

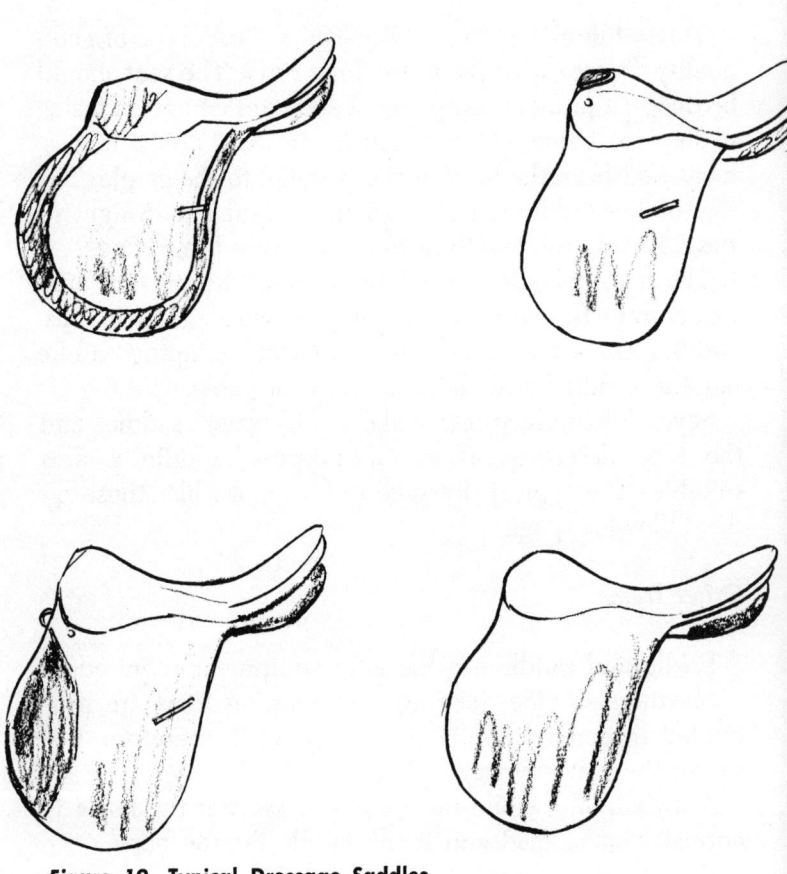

Figure 19. Typical Dressage Saddles

14

Dress

Dress comfortably when you are training. Wear stout shoes, jodhpur boots, Wellington boots, or regular knee-height boots to protect your feet. Knee-height boots will prevent painful chafing of your legs, especially in cold weather. Chafed legs will not provide very effective aids to your horse.

If you don't wear boots and breeches, wear jodhpurs or trousers or "levis" that are fairly tight below the knees, or wear leather straps below the knees to keep the trousers from riding up.

If you are schooling a young, fractious, or nervous horse, wear a hunting cap or other type of "hard hat."

The rules of competition in the first two levels require with respect to dress only that it be "proper."

Generally accepted as "proper" is this:
    A black (or other dark, plain colored) coat
    A white stock and plain pin
    White, preferably, or canary, tan, or grey breeches

Black, knee-height boots
Spurs
A black or dark blue hunting cap, derby, or top hat (only with white breeches, "shadbelly" or "pink" coat)
Leather gloves—unless it is very warm
(See Chapter 10, "The Rules of Competition.")

15

A Reader

The objective and the culmination of training in dressage is to produce a well-schooled horse. Determine the extent to which you have accomplished this by testing yourself and your horse in a competitive ride. (Several appear in Appendix A.) First you will want to do this on your own and then with a coach to make constructive suggestions. Finally, you will want to put your horse and yourself to the real test—an officially judged and scored competitive ride.

Proper preparation would require that you *memorize* the ride in which you are to compete.

Some, however—especially in their first few engagements in competition—in order to avoid panicking and blanking out and to give themselves confidence, feel that they would like to have the ride read or announced. This—for the preliminary and first two levels—is appropriate and permitted by the rules. It is done in from ten to twenty percent of the rides.

The reader stands outside the arena, usually near the middle of one of the long sides. Bear in mind that any mistake made by the reader counts against *you*. As a matter of interest, competitive rides *above* the fourth level—and final competition at any level—*must* be performed from memory.

If you believe that a reader will help or improve your performance, be sure to select one who is experienced in reading dressage tests; and be sure to go over the reading of the ride with him or her.

It is well if the reader abbreviates. For examples: "Change rein at H" says as much as "Change rein H-X-F." If you change rein at H, you will have to pass through X to F; there is no other proper way to go. There is no purpose in reading "Enter at A," since one always does and the rider can be expected at least to know the entering gait. After moving off from the halt and salute, "at C right" or just "Right" should be enough since the gait is seldom changed at that point. (You must "track" so why say that?) "Halt 5 seconds" does not need the addition of the printed "immobile." The halt is always immobile. And so on.

You and your reader should go over the ride together and underline the key words and agree on *when* they are to be announced—neither too soon nor too late.

Again, it is best to memorize the ride.

A READER 89

Figure 20. A "Reader"

16

Using the Judge's Scores and Comments to Improve Your Performance

The men and women who judge your performance in competitive rides are competent and experienced. They know well the standards to be achieved. In what they are looking for, there is no difference. In the judgment of each as to the extent to which their common objective is met, however, there is a difference.

Some judges score low. They never give a 9 or 10 in preliminary, first- and second-level tests and few 8's and 7's. This is because they are scoring you against perfection. Other judges score high. These take into account the ability and training of horse and rider at the beginning levels and want to use the full range of points to provide meaningful comparison. Then, of course, there are judges who fall between the two.

The most valuable assistance available to you in planning improvement is the scores and comments of the judge or judges in competitive tests. Study and record them. Prepare a sheet with all of the movements in the tests along the left side—one or two are published for each level by the American Horse Shows Association each year and these are generally used. On the top of the sheet, list the dates of the tests in which you have been scored. Use one sheet for the scores, another for comments.

Since the range in scores varies somewhat with different judges, it will prove useful—in addition to the actual score for each movement—to record a special symbol to indicate whether your performance was scored: 1) better than satisfactory, 2) satisfactory or sufficient, or 3) less than sufficient. For an example:

$$+ = \text{over } 6$$
$$\# = 5 \text{ or } 6$$
$$- = \text{less than } 5$$

After recording the results for each test you ride, study them and reconcile them with your own impression and the factors *you* believe contributed to a poor performance.

Next, compare the scores and comments on the current (latest) ride with previous rides—and note particularly where you are improving and where you are slipping. Now set up a general and a specific plan for improvement in the areas of weakness.

A tough assignment? Probably. But this procedure will pay off. In a sense, it is the only one that will.

17

Advancing to Higher Levels

When you have received a score of 60 percent or more of the possible points in competitive preliminary or first-level rides three times, determine to bring your score up to 75 percent of the possible points. Do this by careful analysis of the judge's score and comments, to determine where improvement is required, in what respect, and to what extent.

When you have received a score of 75 percent or better twice, start working on the gaits, paces, movements, and figures in the second level. When you have advanced in second-level tests with the same percentages of the possible score as described for the first level, you need—before advancing to work at the third level—to pause and assess the situation.

You need now to review the capabilities of your horse and yourself and the instruction and coaching personnel available to assist you. Certainly, having advanced from the preliminary and first to the second level and then having done well in second-level tests, you should now strive to go on to the more difficult third-level movements and figures and collection at the trot. But this is a bigger step than that from the first to the second level.

So, again, take the time and make the effort required to review the further abilities of your horse and your will to apply yourself to a greater extent to achieve a greater reward and greater satisfaction. Don't be scared—but do recognize the difficulties ahead and prepare well to meet them.

With the right attitude, hard and intelligent application, and, most of all, determination, you can and will advance. GO TO IT!

18

Summary

1. Prepare a regular, systematic, and progressive plan of training in considerable detail—and stick to it.
2. Set daily a realistic objective and insist on its accomplishment.
3. When an objective has been accomplished, encourage your horse with a pat and approving words, terminate the exercise, and do something relaxing away from the training area—walk along a wooded path "on the buckle," canter across open pastures, do something different and relaxing.
4. Be patient; don't be discouraged and, above all, don't lose your temper when progress seems unduly slow and even lacking.
5. Study, observe, and think of experience in terms of progress.
6. Remember that most effective control of a horse is achieved through:
    a. Knowing exactly and in detail what you want to accomplish.

b. Strong and well-placed legs applied with the least pressure that will obtain compliance.

   c. A light hand on the bit.

7. Comparison is important. Do your schooling frequently with others. You will either learn something or know that your plan, activity, and results are better than theirs.

8. Induce a competent friend to observe and coach you from the ground, to tell you what and how you are doing and suggest improvements. Listen to him (or her) with an open mind. You will benefit.

9. After completing your overall training plan—leading to a prescribed ride—concentrate on the weak points.

10. After training has progressed to a complete ride, alternate the complete ride with work on individual gaits, movements, and figures—especially those which you feel need most to be improved.

11. To assist committing to memory a test ride you are about to enter, construct or draw a small arena to scale—1" = 10 feet or 5 feet, or—if you have available a dining-room table—1" = 2 feet.

12. Pick up pointers from others; watch critically as many rides as you can and ask meaningful questions of experienced riders.

Appendixes A, B, and C

APPENDIX A

Preliminary Level Dressage Test

PURPOSE: To introduce the rider and horse to the basic principles of dressage competition.

CONDITIONS: a) To be ridden in a *plain snaffle* with or without dropped noseband.
b) Arena size: 20 m. x 40 m. (66' x 132').
c) Time allowed: No time limit.

SCORING: The test is to be judged on the overall picture of horse and rider and evaluated with one score based on 100%.

No. _____ Event _____ Date _____
Horse _____ Rider _____

		TEST	REMARKS
1	A	Enter working trot (rising).	
	X	Halt. Salute. Proceed working trot (rising).	
	C	Track to the right.	
2	H	Working trot (sitting).	
	C	Circle right, width of arena.	
	C	Ordinary canter, right lead. Circle width of arena.	

	TEST	REMARKS
3 A M-X-K K	Working trot (rising). Change rein. Working trot (sitting).	
4 A A	Circle left width of arena. Ordinary canter, left lead. Circle width of arena.	
5 E A X	Working trot (sitting). Down center line. Halt. Salute. Leave arena free walk.	
6	GENERAL IMPRESSIONS Paces (regularity and freedom).	
7	Impulsion.	
8	Obedience, lightness and suppleness of horse.	
9	Position and seat of rider. Correct use of aids.	

Evaluation _____
Judge's Signature: _____

Preliminary Level Dressage Test

PURPOSE: To introduce the rider and horse to the basic principles of dressage competition.

CONDITIONS: a) To be ridden in a *plain snaffle* with or without dropped noseband.
b) Arena size: 20 m. x 40 m. (66' x 132').
c) Time allowed: No time limit.

SCORING:
10 Excellent
9 Very Good
8 Good
7 Fairly Good
6 Satisfactory
5 Sufficient
4 Insufficient
3 Fairly Bad
2 Bad
1 Very Bad
0 Not Performed or Fall of Horse or Rider

ELEMENTARY DRESSAGE

PENALTIES: Errors: 1st error, 2 points; 2nd error, 5 points; 3rd error, elimination; leaving arena, elimination. (When test is part of a combined event, 3rd error 10 points; 4th error, elimination).

No. _____ Event _____ Date _____

Horse _____ Rider _____

	TEST	POINTS	REMARKS
1 A X C	Enter working trot (sitting). Halt. Salute. Proceed working trot (sitting). Track to the left.		
2 H-X-F	Change rein, working trot (rising).		
3 A	Circle right, width of arena.		
4 K-X-M	Change rein.		
5 C	Circle left, width of arena.		
6 C-H-E	Working trot (sitting).		
7 E A	Halt, 5 sec., proceed ordinary walk. Working trot (sitting). Develop ordinary canter between F and B.		
8 B B-H	Circle left width of arena. Ordinary canter.		
9 H-X-F F-E	Change rein, working trot (sitting). Working trot (sitting).		
10 E C	Halt, 5 sec., proceed ordinary walk. Working trot (sitting). Develop ordinary canter between M and B.		
11 B F-K	Circle right, width of arena. Ordinary canter.		

	TEST	POINTS	REMARKS
12 K-X-M	Change rein, working trot (sitting).		
M-H	Working trot (sitting).		
13 H-K-A	Working trot (rising).		
14 A	Down center line; at D halt 5 sec., proceed at ordinary walk.		
G	Halt; salute, leave arena free walk.		
	GENERAL IMPRESSIONS		
15	Paces (regularity and freedom).		
16	Impulsion.		
17	Obedience, lightness and suppleness of horse.		
18	Position and seat of rider. Correct use of aids.		

Points to be Deducted:

Total Points _____
Error _____
Final Score _____

Judge's Signature _____

First Level Dressage Test

PURPOSE: To determine that the correct foundation has been laid for successful training of the riding horse; that the horse moves freely forward in a relaxed manner and with rhythm, its spine always parallel to the track of the prescribed movement; that it accepts the bit and obeys the simple aids of the rider.

CONDITIONS: a) To be ridden in a *plain snaffle* with or without dropped noseband.
b) Arena size: 20 m. x 40 m. (66' x 132') or 20 m. x 60 m. (66' x 198').
c) Time allowed: 6½ minutes (small arena), 8 minutes (large arena).

SCORING: 10 Excellent   5 Sufficient
           9 Very Good   4 Insufficient
           8 Good   3 Fairly Bad
           7 Fairly Good   2 Bad
           6 Satisfactory   1 Very Bad
           0 Not Performed or Fall of Horse or Rider

PENALTIES: Time: 1 point for each commenced 5 seconds overtime.
Errors: 1st error, 2 points; 2nd error, 5 points; 3rd error, elimination; leaving arena, elimination. (When test is part of a combined event, 3rd error 10 points; 4th error, elimination).

Contestant's Number_____ Rider_____

Horse_____

	TEST	POINTS	REMARKS
1 A X C	Enter working trot (sitting). Halt. Salute, Proceed ordinary trot (sitting). Track to the right.		
2 F	Half circle right, 10 m. (33') diameter, returning to track at B.		
3 C	Circle left 10 m. (33') diameter.		
4 K	Half circle left, 10 m. (33') diameter, returning to track at E.		
5 C	Circle right, 10 m. (33') diameter.		
6 M-X-K X	Change rein, Halt (5 seconds). Proceed working trot (sitting).		
7 A F-X-H H	Ordinary walk. Change rein free walk. Ordinary walk.		

	TEST	POINTS	REMARKS
8 C A	Working trot (sitting). One circle, 20 m. (width of arena), ordinary canter, right lead.		
9 M-X-K	Change rein, at X, working trot (sitting)		
10 A B	Ordinary walk. Working trot (sitting).		
11 A	One circle, 20 m. (width of arena), ordinary canter, left lead.		
12 H-X-F	Change rein, at X, working trot (sitting).		
13 K-X-M M	Change rein, extended trot (sitting). Working trot (sitting).		
14 F-X-H H	Change rein, extended trot (rising). Working trot (sitting).		
15 A G	Down center line. Halt. Salute. Leave arena free walk.		
16	GENERAL IMPRESSIONS Paces (regularity and freedom).		
17	Impulsion.		
18	Obedience, lightness and suppleness of horse.		
19	Position and seat of rider. Correct use of aids.		

Total Points _____
Points to be Deducted: Time _____
Error _____
Final Score _____

Judge's Signature _____

First Level Dressage Test

PURPOSE: To determine that the correct foundation is being laid for successful training of the riding horse; that the horse moves freely forward in a relaxed manner and with rhythm, its spine always parallel to the track of the prescribed movement; that it accepts the bit and obeys simple aids of the rider.

CONDITIONS:
a) To be ridden in a *plain snaffle* with or without dropped noseband.
b) Arena size: 20 m. x 40 m. (66' x 132').
c) Time allowed: 6 minutes (small arena); 7 minutes (large arena).

SCORING:
10 Excellent
9 Very Good
8 Good
7 Fairly Good
6 Satisfactory
5 Sufficient
4 Insufficient
3 Fairly Bad
2 Bad
1 Very Bad
0 Not Performed or Fall of Horse or Rider

PENALTIES:
Time: 1 point for each commenced 5 seconds overtime.
Errors: 1st error, 2 points; 2nd error, 5 points; 3rd error, elimination; leaving arena, elimination. (When test is part of a combined event, 3rd error, 10 points; 4th error, elimination).

No. _____ Event _____ Date _____
Horse _____ Rider _____

	TEST	POINTS	REMARKS
1 A X C	Enter working trot (sitting). Halt. Salute. Proceed working trot (sitting). Track to the right.		
2 F	Half circle right, 10 meters (33') diameter, returning to track at B.		
3 C	Circle left 10 meters (33') diameter.		

	TEST	POINTS	REMARKS
4 K	Half circle left, 10 meters (33′) diameter, returning to track at E.		
5 C	Circle right 10 meters (33′) diameter.		
6 M-X-K	Change rein.		
7 A F-X-H H	Ordinary walk. Change rein, free walk. Ordinary walk.		
8 M F A	Working trot (sitting). Ordinary canter, right lead. Circle width of arena.		
9 K-X-M	Change rein, change of lead at M through trot.		
10 K M C	Working trot (sitting). Ordinary canter, left lead. Circle width of arena.		
11 H-X-F	Change rein, change of lead at F through trot.		
12 H M-X-K K	Working trot (sitting). Change rein, extended trot (rising). Working trot (sitting).		
13 F-X-H H	Change rein, extended trot (sitting). Working trot (sitting).		
14 C	Halt (5 sec.). Proceed working trot (sitting).		
15 A G	Down center line. Halt. Salute. Leave arena free walk.		
	GENERAL IMPRESSIONS		
16	Paces (regularity and freedom).		
17	Impulsion.		
18	Obedience, lightness and suppleness of horse.		

	TEST	POINTS	REMARKS
19	Position and seat of rider. Correct use of aids.		

Total points _____
Points to be Deducted: Time _____
Error _____
Final Score _____

Judge's Signature: _____

First Level Dressage Test

PURPOSE: To determine that the correct foundation is being laid for successful training of the riding horse; that the horse moves freely forward in a relaxed manner and with rhythm, its spine always parallel to the track of the prescribed movement; that it accepts the bit and obeys simple aids of the rider.

CONDITIONS:
a) To be ridden in a plain snaffle with or without dropped noseband.
b) Arena size: 20 m. x 40 m. (66′ x 132′).
c) Time allowed: 6 minutes (small arena); 7 minutes (large arena).

SCORING:
10 Excellent
9 Very Good
8 Good
7 Fairly Good
6 Satisfactory
5 Sufficient
4 Insufficient
3 Fairly Bad
2 Bad
1 Very Bad
0 Not Performed or Fall of Horse or Rider

PENALTIES: Time: 1 point for each commenced 5 seconds overtime.
Errors: 1st error, 2 points; 2nd error, 5 points; 3rd error, elimination; leaving arena, elimination. (When test is part of a combined event, 3rd error, 10 points; 4th error, elimination).

No. _____ Event _____ Date _____
Horse _____ Rider _____

APPENDIXES A, B, AND C

	TEST	POINTS	REMARKS
1 A X C	Enter working trot (sitting). Halt. Salute. Proceed working trot (sitting). Track to the left.		
2 H-X-F	Change rein.		
3 K-X-M M	Change rein, working trot (rising). Working trot (sitting).		
4 K	Half circle, left 10 meters, (33′) diameter, returning to track at E.		
5 H	Half circle, right 10 meters, (33′) diameter, returning to track at E.		
6 K A	Ordinary canter, left lead. Circle width of arena. Once around.		
7 F-X-H	Change rein, at X, working trot (sitting).		
8 H	Ordinary canter, right lead.		
9 A E	Working trot (sitting). Halt, (5 sec.). Proceed working trot (sitting).		
10 H C	Ordinary canter, right lead. Circle, width of arena. Once around.		
11 M-X-K	Change rein, at X, working trot (sitting).		
12 K	Ordinary canter, left lead.		
13 C H-X-F F	Working trot (sitting). Change rein, extended trot (rising). Working trot (sitting).		
14 K-X-M M	Change rein, extended trot (sitting). Working trot (sitting).		

	TEST	POINTS	REMARKS
15 C H-X-F F	Ordinary walk. Change rein, free walk. Ordinary walk.		
16 A D G	Down center line. Working trot (sitting). Halt. Salute. Leave arena free walk.		
	GENERAL IMPRESSIONS		
17	Paces (regularity and freedom).		
18	Impulsion.		
19	Obedience, lightness and suppleness of horse.		
20	Position and seat of rider. Correct use of aids.		

Points to be Deducted:

Total Points _____
Time _____
Error _____
Final Score _____

Judge's Signature: _____

Second Level Dressage Test

PURPOSE: To determine that the horse has acquired, in addition to those qualities of the first level tests, a degree of suppleness, balance, and impulsion.

CONDITIONS: a) To be ridden in a *plain snaffle* with or without dropped noseband.
b) Arena size: 20 m. x 40 m. (66' x 132') or 20 m. x 60 m. (66' x 198').
c) Time allowed: 7 minutes (small arena); 8½ minutes (large arena).

SCORING: 10 Excellent   5 Sufficient
          9 Very Good   4 Insufficient
          8 Good   3 Fairly Bad
          7 Fairly Good   2 Bad
          6 Satisfactory   1 Very Bad
              0 Not Performed or Fall of Horse or Rider

PENALTIES: Time: 1 point for each commenced 5 seconds overtime.
Errors: 1st error, 2 points; 2nd error, 5 points; 3rd error, elimination; leaving arena, elimination. (When test is part of a combined event, 3rd error, 10 points; 4th error, elimination).

Contestant's Number_____ Rider_____

Horse_____

	TEST	POINTS	REMARKS
1 A X C	Enter working trot (sitting). Halt. Salute. Proceed working trot (sitting). Track to the left.		
2 E X B	Turn left. Circle left, 10 m. (33') diameter followed by a Circle right, 10 m. Track right.		
3 A-C	Serpentine of 4 loops, 5 m. (16'6") each side of center line.		
4 C H-X-F F	Ordinary walk, track left. Change rein, free walk. Ordinary walk.		
5 A	Halt. Rein back 4 steps. Proceed ordinary walk.		
6 K	Half turn on haunches (right).		
7 A F-B	Working trot (sitting). Shoulder-in.		
8 C H	Ordinary walk. Half turn on haunches (left).		
9 C M-B	Working trot (sitting). Shoulder-in.		

ELEMENTARY DRESSAGE

	TEST	POINTS	REMARKS
10 K H K	Ordinary canter, right lead. Half circle, 10 m. (33′) diameter, returning to track at E. Change of lead through the trot.		
11 M F	Half circle, 10 m. (33′) diameter, returning to track at B. Change of lead through the trot.		
12 K-H H	Working trot (sitting). Ordinary canter, right lead.		
13 M-X-K	Change rein, change of lead through the trot at X.		
14 A F	Working trot (rising). Ordinary canter, left lead.		
15 C H-X-F F	Working trot (sitting). Change rein, extended trot (sitting). Working trot (sitting).		
16 K-X-M M	Change rein, extended trot (rising). Working trot (sitting).		
17 A X	Turn down center line. Halt. Salute. Leave arena free walk.		
18	GENERAL IMPRESSIONS Paces (regularity and freedom).		
19	Impulsion.		
20	Obedience, lightness and suppleness of horse.		
21	Position and seat of rider. Correct use of aids.		

Points to be Deducted:

Total Points _____
Time _____
Error _____
Final Score _____

Judge's Signature _____

Second Level Dressage Test

PURPOSE: To determine that the horse has acquired, in addition to those qualities of the First Level, a degree of suppleness, balance and impulsion.

CONDITIONS:
a) To be ridden in a *plain snaffle* with or without dropped noseband.
b) Arena size: 20 m. x 40 m. (66' x 132').
c) Time allowed: 8 minutes (small arena); 9 minutes (large arena).

SCORING:
10 Excellent   5 Sufficient
9 Very Good   4 Insufficient
8 Good   3 Fairly Bad
7 Fairly Good   2 Bad
6 Satisfactory   1 Very Bad
0 Not Performed or Fall of Horse or Rider

PENALTIES:
Time: 1 point for each commenced 5 seconds overtime.
Errors: 1st error, 2 points; 2nd error, 5 points; 3rd error, elimination; leaving arena, elimination. (When test is part of a combined event, 3rd error, 10 points; 4th error, elimination).

No. _____ Event _____ Date _____
Horse _____ Rider _____

	TEST	POINTS	REMARKS
1 A X C	Enter working trot (sitting). Halt. Salute. Proceed working trot (sitting). Track to the left.		
2 A X	Down center line. Circle left, 10 meters (33') diameter, followed immediately by a circle right, 10 meters (33') diameter.		
3 C H-K K	Track to the left. Working trot (rising). Working trot (sitting).		

	TEST	POINTS	REMARKS
4 F-B B-H	Shoulder-in. Change rein across half arena, ordinary trot (sitting).		
5 M-F F	Working trot (rising). Working trot (sitting).		
6 K-E E-M	Shoulder-in. Change rein across half arena, working trot (sitting).		
7 C H-X-F F	Ordinary walk. Change rein, free walk. Ordinary walk.		
8 A	Half turn on haunches (right).		
9 A-B B	Ordinary walk. Half turn on haunches (left).		
10 F A H K	Working trot (sitting). Ordinary canter, right lead. Half circle, 10 meters (33′) diameter, returning to track at E. Working trot (sitting).		
11 A M F	Ordinary canter, left lead. Half circle, 10 meters (33′) diameter, returning to track at B. Working trot (sitting).		
12 A	Ordinary canter, right lead.		
13 M-X-K	Change rein, at X, working trot (sitting).		
14 A	Ordinary canter (left lead).		
15 C E X B	Working trot. Turn left. Halt. Rein back four steps. Proceed working trot (sitting). Turn right.		

	TEST	POINTS	REMARKS
16 K-X-M	Change rein, extended trot (rising).		
M	Working trot (sitting).		
17 H-X-F	Change rein, extended trot (sitting).		
F	Working trot (sitting).		
18 A	Down center line.		
G	Halt. Salute. Leave arena free walk.		
	GENERAL IMPRESSIONS		
19	Paces (regularity and freedom).		
20	Impulsion.		
21	Obedience, lightness and suppleness of horse.		
22	Position and seat of rider. Correct use of aids.		

Points to be Deducted: Total Points _____
Time _____
Error _____
Final Score _____

Judge's Signature: _____

Second Level Dressage Test

PURPOSE: To determine that the horse has acquired, in addition to those qualities of the First Level, a degree of suppleness, balance and impulsion.

CONDITIONS: a) To be ridden in a plain sniffle with or without dropped noseband.
b) Arena size: 20 m. x 40 m. (66' x 132').
c) Time allowed: 8 minutes (small arena); 9 minutes (large arena).

SCORING:
10 Excellent   5 Sufficient
9 Very Good   4 Insufficient
8 Good   3 Fairly Bad
7 Fairly Good   2 Bad
6 Satisfactory   1 Very Bad
0 Not Performed or Fall of Horse or Rider.

ELEMENTARY DRESSAGE

PENALTIES: Time: 1 point for each commenced 5 seconds overtime.
Errors: 1st error, 2 points; 2nd error, 5 points; 3rd error, elimination; leaving arena, elimination. (When test is part of a combined event, 3rd error, 10 points; 4th error, elimination).

No. _____ Event _____ Date _____
Horse _____ Rider _____

	TEST	POINTS	REMARKS
1 A X C	Enter working trot (sitting). Halt. Salute. Proceed working trot (sitting). Track to the left.		
2 A-C	Serpentine of 4 loops, width of arena.		
3 C B X E	Track to the right. Turn right. Halt (5 seconds). Proceed working trot (sitting). Track to the left.		
4 F-B B B-M	Shoulder-in. Circle 8 meters (26') diameter. Shoulder-in.		
5 C H-X-F F	Working trot (sitting). Change rein, extended trot (rising). Working trot (sitting).		
6 K-E E E-H	Shoulder-in. Circle 8 meters (26') diameter. Shoulder-in.		
7 H M-X-K K	Working trot (sitting). Change rein, extended trot (sitting). Working trot (sitting).		
8 F B	Ordinary walk. Half turn on haunches (left).		

APPENDIXES A, B, AND C

	TEST	POINTS	REMARKS
9 F A X	Ordinary canter, right lead. Down center line. Circle right, 10 meters (33') diameter.		
10 G C K E	Working trot (sitting). Track to the right. Ordinary walk. Half turn on haunches (right).		
11 K A X	Ordinary canter, left lead. Down center line. Circle left, 10 meters (33') diameter.		
12 X G C	Working trot (sitting). Ordinary canter, right lead. Track to the right.		
13 M-X-K K	Change rein. Change lead through trot.		
14 F-X-H H	Change rein. Change lead through trot.		
15 C M-X-K K	Ordinary walk. Change rein, free walk. Ordinary walk.		
16 A B X E	Working trot (sitting). Turn left. Halt. Rein back four steps. Proceed working trot (sitting). Turn left.		
17 A G	Down center line. Halt. Salute. Leave arena free walk.		
	GENERAL IMPRESSIONS		
18	Paces (regularity and freedom).		
19	Impulsion.		
20	Obedience, lightness and suppleness of horse.		

	TEST	POINTS	REMARKS
21	Position and seat of rider. Correct use of aids.		

Points to be Deducted:

Total Points _____
Time _____
Error _____
Final Score _____

Judge's Signature: _____

APPENDIX B

Conversion Table

Meters—Yards—Feet—Inches

METERS	FEET	FEET	METERS
1	3′3⅓″	1	.305
.75	2′6″	2′6″	.75
5	16′6″	16′6″	5
6	20	20	6
8	26	26	8
10	33	33	10
20	66	66	20
40	132	132	40
60	198	198	60
100	109.3 yards	100 yards	91.44

APPENDIX C

The Rein Effects

(Reprinted from "Horsemanship and Riding," written by the author for The Encyclopaedia Britannica)

Reins.—The rider's hands restrain and guide the horse through the application and relaxation of pressure and tension on the bit in the horse's mouth by means of the reins. The controlling principle in the use of the reins is to push the horse onto the bit with the legs and not to pull the horse back with the bit. The reins are used in five basic actions or effects:

APPENDIXES A, B, AND C 117

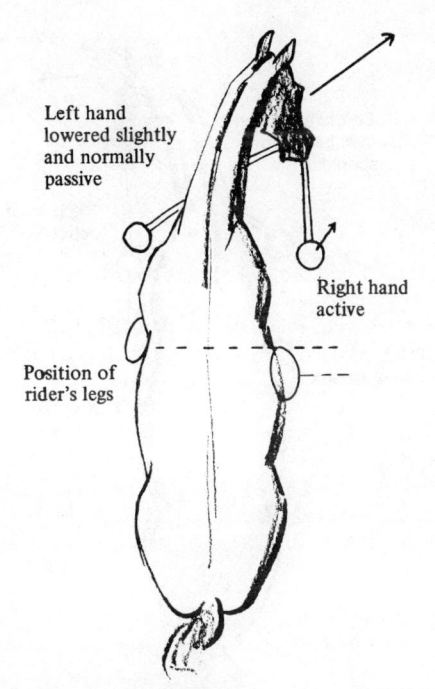

Fig. **A—Right leading (opening) rein**

Leading (or opening) rein.—The rein is carried to the side and slightly to the front with no tension to the rear; used to turn the horse to the right or left on a large circle.

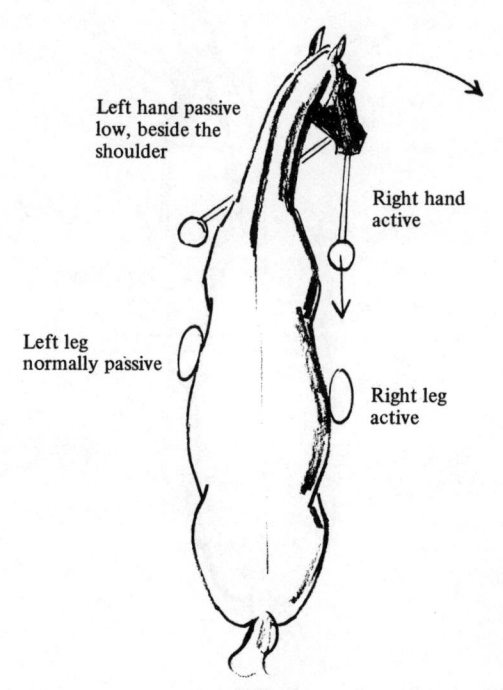

Fig. B—**Right direct rein of opposition**

Direct rein of opposition.—The rein is held slightly to the side and drawn to the rear; used to turn the horse to the right or left on a small and sharp circle.

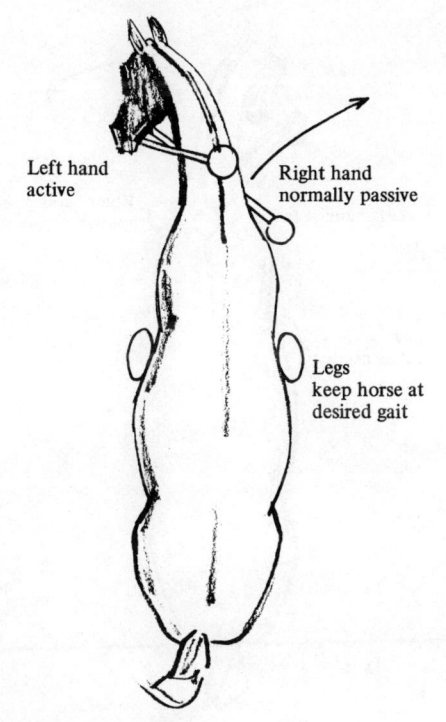

Fig. C—Left bearing (neck) rein

Bearing (or neck) rein.—The rein is raised and carried forward against the neck toward the opposite side; used to change direction when the reins are held in one hand and the change is made at speed. (In the early stages of training this is usually combined with a leading rein on the opposite side.)

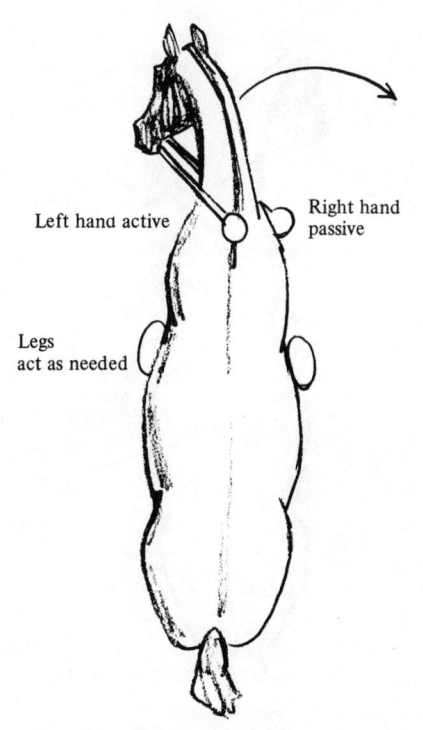

Fig. D—**Left indirect rein of opposition, in front of withers**

Indirect rein of opposition—in front of the withers.—
One hand is raised slightly to carry the rein across the horse's neck toward the opposite side—in front of the withers—with pressure to that side and to the rear. The other hand is passive.

If the left indirect rein is used, the horse's muzzle is turned slightly to the left and rear (while the left hand is carried to the right across the horse's neck, with tension to the right rear, causing the horse to turn to the right). This rein is used when the horse, moving, is to turn

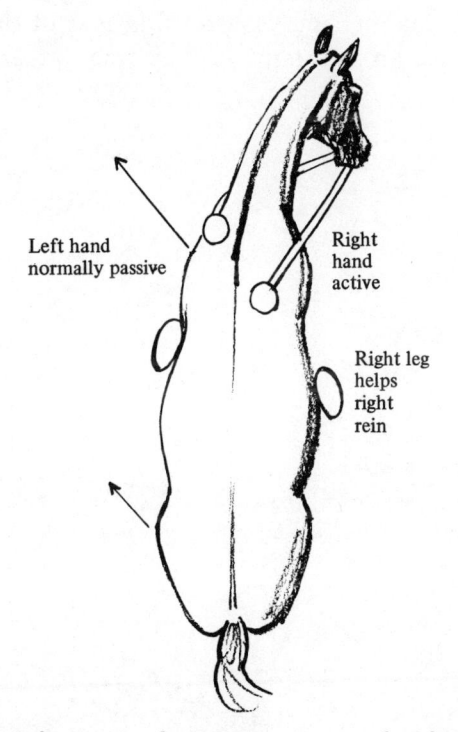

Fig. E—**Right indirect rein of opposition, in rear of withers**

sharply—the degree of sharpness of the turn depending on the amount of pressure on the rein.

Indirect rein of opposition—in rear of the withers.— One hand applies pressure toward the rear in the direction of the horse's opposite hip, but does not cross the neck. The other hand is passive. The horse's head is turned to the desired side and rear, its neck and spine curved to that side, forcing the mass of the horse against the opposite hip and hind leg, and increasing the weight borne by the opposite shoulder. This rein effect is used to move the horse in the opposite direction while advancing. For example, if the right indirect rein is applied in rear of the withers, the horse would move to the left front at an angle of about 45°.

Index

Advancing to higher levels, 92
American Horse Shows Association (A.H.S.A.), 16
Arena, dressage, 19, 20

Back, rein, 23, 34, 62
Bandages, 71
Basic requirements, 22
Bearing (or neck) rein, 83, 119
Bit, on the, 25
Bits, 71, 72, 82
Breastplate, 83
Bridle, 83

Cadence, 25
Calm, 25
Canter, ordinary, 22, 28, 33, 34, 59
Center line, down, 39
Change of lead (or leg), 22, 34, 61
Change rein, 22, 44, 69
Change of gait and pace, 39
Circle, 33-foot diameter training aid, 66
Circles, 22, 41, 66
Classification of tests, 16, 75
Comments by judges, typical, 79
Competition, rules of, 71
Competitive ride, preparation for, 80

Conversion table—meters, yards, feet, inches, 115
Corners, turning, 22, 39, 40

Details of the gaits, movements, and figures, 27
Direct rein of opposition, 118
Disqualifications, summary of, 75
Down center line, 39
Dress, 71, 75, 85
Dressage arena, 19, 20
Dressage saddles, typical, 83, 84
Dressage tests, preliminary, 16, 96, 97; first level, 16, 99, 102, 104; second level, 16, 106, 109, 111
Dressage, what is?, 15; what does it accomplish?, 17
Dropped noseband, 71, 73

Elimination (disqualification), 75
Errors, 74, 75
Extended trot, 22, 31, 59
Extended walk, 23, 29, 57

Fall of horse or rider, 73, 75
F.E.I. (Fédération Equestre Internationale), 16
Figures, 24, 39
First level test, 16, 75, 99, 102, 104
Fourth level test, 16
Free walk, 22, 29, 58

123

Gait and pace, 28, 54
Gaits, 24, 28
Grand Prix, 16

Half circle (turn) and return to the track, 22, 41, 68
Half turn on the haunches, 23, 36, 63
Halt, 22, 27, 54
Hands, seat and, 46
Haunches, turn on the, 23, 36, 63
Higher levels, advancing to, 92
Hints (summary), 94
Horses, 52, 71
How you are scored, 77

Improve your performance, using judge's score and comments to, 90
Impulsion, 25
Indirect rein of opposition, in front of withers, 120; in rear of withers, 121
Intermediare, 16

Judge's scores and comments, using, 79, 90

Lameness, marked, 75
Lead (leg), change of, 22, 34, 61
Leading (or opening) rein, 117
Leaving the arena, 74, 75

Marked lameness, 75
Martingales, 71, 83
Meters, conversion to yards, feet, inches, 115
Mount, suitable, 52
Movements, 24, 34

Neck (or bearing) rein, 83, 117
Noseband, 71, 73

On the bit, 25
Ordinary canter, 22, 28, 33, 34, 59
Ordinary walk, 22, 28, 29, 56

Pace, 28, 54
Plan for training, 54
Precision, 24
Preliminary level test, 16, 75, 96, 97
Preparation for a competitive ride, 80
Prix St. Georges, 16
Promptness, 24
Proper dress, 71, 75, 85

Qualities that apply to all gaits, figures and movements, 24

Reader, 73, 87, 89
Reading, 73, 87, 89
References (books and pamphlets), 76
Rein back, 23, 34, 62
Rein, bearing (or neck), 83, 119
Rein, direct, of opposition, 118
Rein effects, 116
Rein, indirect of opposition—in front of withers, 120; in rear of withers, 121
Rein, leading (or opening), 117
Reins: bearing, 83; running, 83; side, 83
Requirements, basic, 22
Rules of competition, 71
Running reins, 83

Saddles, typical dressage, 83, 84
Score, tied, 75
Scored, how you are, 77
Seat and hands, 46
Seat: dressage, 46, 48; hunter, 49; saddle, 50; stock, 51
Second level test, 16, 75, 106, 109, 111
Serpentines, 23, 42, 68
Shoulder-in, 23, 36, 64
Side reins, 83
Small dressage arena, 19, 20
Snaffle bits, 71, 72, 80
Suitable mount, 52

Summary, 94; of disqualifications, 75

Tack, 82
Tests: preliminary, 16, 75, 96, 97; first level, 16, 75, 99, 102, 104; second level, 16, 75, 106, 109, 111; third level, 16; fourth level, 16; classification of, 16, 75
Third level test, 16
Tied score, 75
Time, 74
Training, plan for, 54
Transitions, 39
Trot: extended, 22, 31, 59; ordinary, 31; working, 22, 31, 58
Turning a corner, 22, 39
Turn on the haunches, 23, 36, 63

Typical comments by judges, 79
Typical dressage saddles, 83, 84

Using the judge's scores and comments, 90

Voice, 73

Walk: extended, 23, 29, 57; free, 22, 29, 58; ordinary, 22, 28, 29, 56
What does dressage accomplish?, 17
What is dressage?, 15
Whips, 71
Working trot, 22, 31, 58

Yards, conversion to meters, 115